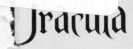

Dracula

Kenneth Brodey

Illustrated by Gianni De Conno

Editor: Daniela Penzavalle
Design and art direction: Nadia Maestri
Computer graphics: Simona Corniola
Picture research: Laura Lagomarsino

© 2009   Black Cat

First edition: February 2009

Picture credits
Cideb Archive; © Hulton-Deutsch Collection/CORBIS: 4;
© Bettmann/CORBIS: 6, 136, 137; De Agostini Picture Library: 8;
© Underwood & Underwood/CORBIS: 41; Album: 43, 135;
© Visuals Unlimited/Corbis: 77; Jonathan Barry/Getty
Images/Laura Ronchi: 117.

We would be happy to receive your comments and
suggestions, and give you any other information concerning
our material.

www.blackcat-cideb.com

ISBN 978-88-530-0960-9   Book + CD

Printed in Italy by Litoprint, Genoa

Contents

Chapters 1, 3, 4, 5, 8 are recorded on the accompanying CD.
Chapters 2, 6, 7 are downloadable from our website:
www.cideb.it or www.blackcat-cideb.com.

These symbols indicate the beginning and end of the passages
linked to the listening activities.

www.blackcat-cideb.com passage downloadable from our site.

Bram Stoker (about 1880).

About the Author

Bram Stoker, who was born in Clontarf, Ireland in 1847, grew up listening to great horror stories. He was a sickly boy and his mother often helped him pass the time by telling Irish tales of banshees, [1] demons and ghouls. [2]

1. **banshees** : women spirits in Irish folklore that appeared screaming in front of the house of a person who was dying.
2. **ghouls** [gu:lz] : evil spirits that rob graves and eat the dead bodies.

Mrs Stoker was also a writer, a social worker [3] and a feminist. She thought that the world's problems could be solved by 'equalising the sexes'. [4] At first Bram accepted his mother's views, but when he wrote *Dracula* he had already changed his mind. As you will see for yourselves, Bram thought women should be the servants of men. In fact, the character Mina can be seen as Bram's ideal woman: courageous and intelligent, but always working to help her man.

Bram's father, a civil servant [5] in Dublin, transmitted to Bram his passion for the theatre, a passion that influenced Bram's life even more than his passion for horror.

Bram went to Trinity College, after graduating, he worked for several years for the Irish civil service. He even used his own and his father's great experience to compose a book called *The Duties of Clerks of Petty Sessions in Ireland*. But Bram continued to pursue his real passion, the theatre.

He spent all his free time going to the theatre and writing reviews [6] for different newspapers. In 1867 Bram saw for the first time his own personal 'Dracula', the man who would suck out all of Bram's life and financial blood. This personal Dracula was Henry Irving, a great actor, the man who made acting into the respectable profession it is today.

After seeing Irving for the first time, Bram began to praise [7] him in reviews and in December 1878 he became Irving's business manager.

3. **social worker** : someone who worked to make social conditions better, especially for the poor.
4. **equalising the sexes** : making men and women equal, i.e., giving the same rights to men and women.
5. **civil servant** : someone who works for the government.
6. **reviews** : articles in which he gave his opinion of what he saw.
7. **to praise** : to say very good things about.

He worked with complete devotion for this tyrannical actor for twenty-seven years. Bram made very little money, often worked fifteen hours a day, and sometimes wrote as many as fifty letters a day for Irving. Bram's death certificate says that he died of 'exhaustion'. And yet, even though Bram received little money for his work and was often in debt, he lived an exciting life. Irving ran a club in the back of his theatre, and after the actor's performance all sorts of people came to have dinner with Irving. Two things held these varied

Sir Henry Irving (1877).

people together: a love of good food and a love of good stories. Bram himself was a great storyteller, and both the food and tales of Irving's club were, according to Bram himself, the beginning of his greatest tale, *Dracula*. He said, 'The idea came to me in a nightmare. One evening I was dining with Henry Irving when I ate too much dressed [8] crab [9] and I spent all night long dreaming

8. **dressed** : with sauce.

9. **crab** :

these weird [10] dreams about a dead/alive man preying on the living!'

In the first drafts of Bram's novel, Count Dracula was called 'Count Wampyr', but in 1897 Bram read a book by William Wilkinson about Vlad Tepes, a cruel Transylvanian count also called Dracula, a name which means either 'Dragon', or by extension, 'the Devil'. He was never considered a vampire, but he was known for his incredible cruelty in war. He fought against the Turks, and when he won a battle he impaled [11] his prisoners. In fact he became known as the 'Impaler'.

But the Count Dracula of the novel has little in common with this cruel count: rather, Bram's vampire is a clear descendent of the Gothic tradition in English and European literature. Gothic novels often had old castles and ghosts, and of course, lots of primitive passions. All sorts of psychological conflicts which could not be discussed in any other way could come out in Gothic novels.

Dracula is full of passion and real fears; fears that are still very much alive today: the fear of death and the dead, and the fear of sexual passions. Bram himself wrote that 'the only emotions which in the long run hurt are those arising from sex impulses...'

In *Dracula* people are buried, but we are never sure if they are really dead. The women in this book fear Count Dracula but at the same time they can feel his great charm, and the men hesitate before the beauty of the women vampires they should kill.

Bram Stoker's book has been interpreted in a myriad of ways, and his character Count Dracula has appeared in more than 200 films.

10. **weird** : strange and supernatural.
11. **impaled** : pushed something sharp through their bodies.

Vlad IV Prince of Wallachia, known as 'The Impaler' (15th century).

Everybody knows who he is, from small children to adults without ever having read the novel. Who doesn't know that the Count sleeps in a coffin, drinks blood, turns into a bat, hates garlic and dies if you drive [12] a stake [13] through his heart? But of course, Count Dracula, who first appeared in 1897, is eternally young, and will, in one form or another, haunt our lives for many more years to come.

12. **drive** : push through with force.
13. **a stake** : ⎯⎯⎯⎯⎯

Bram Stoker also wrote other books of horror:

The Snake's Pass (1890), *The Jewel of Seven Stars* (1903), *The Lady of the Shroud* (1909) and *The Lair of the White Worm* (1911).

He died in 1912.

1 Comprehension check

Say whether the following statements are true (T) or false (F), and then correct the false ones.

		T	F
1	Bram Stoker had a healthy childhood.	☐	☐
2	He did not like the stories his mother told him.	☐	☐
3	Bram's mother was an independent woman with strong opinions.	☐	☐
4	Mina, one of the characters in *Dracula*, is almost exactly like Bram's mother.	☐	☐
5	Bram's first job after university was with the government.	☐	☐
6	Henry Irving had an important role in the history of the theatre.	☐	☐
7	Working for Henry Irving was difficult but very stimulating.	☐	☐
8	Bram made a lot of money working for Henry Irving.	☐	☐
9	Bram got the idea for *Dracula* from his own dreams.	☐	☐
10	The historical Count Dracula was an incredibly violent man.	☐	☐
11	The fictional Count Dracula was closely modelled on the historical Count Dracula.	☐	☐
12	*Dracula* talks about things that still frighten us today.	☐	☐
13	The character Dracula has only appeared in a few films.	☐	☐
14	Most people know who Count Dracula is, even if they have not read the novel.	☐	☐

Mina

Renfield

Dr Seward

Jonathan

Quincey

Arthur

Van Helsing

Lucy

Dracula

The Characters

Before you read

1 **What do you know about Dracula?**
Work with a partner. Write everything you know about Count Dracula and vampires, then present your ideas to the class. Think about the following:

- looks
- powers
- way of talking
- likes
- dislikes
- where he lives
- how he can be destroyed

2 **Listening**
Listen to the first part of Chapter One. For questions 1-9, complete the sentences.

1 Jonathan learned about his future travel in ....

2 The eve of St George's Day frightened ....

3 After Jonathan received the crucifix, he felt ....

4 Jonathan was no longer .... during the journey.

5 Once the sun went down, the passengers wanted the coach to ....

6 They arrived at the Borgo Pass .... early.

7 A moment before the other coached arrived, the horses ....

8 When the strange driver heard a passenger say, 'The dead travel fast,' he ....

9 Jonathan had the impression that the strange coach .... in a big circle.

The Dead Travel Fast

Jonathan Harker's Diary (written in Bistritz)

3 May

I left Munich for Transylvania on 1 May. When I arrived there at the Golden Krone Hotel, the landlady,[1] a very friendly old woman, welcomed me at the door of the hotel and said, 'The English gentleman?' 'Yes,' I replied, and she gave me this letter:

> *My Friend,*
> *welcome to the Carpathians. Sleep well tonight. At three tomorrow a coach will start for Bukovina. A place on it is kept for you. At the Borgo Pass my coach will wait for you and bring you to me.*
> *Your friend,*
> *Dracula*

---

1. **landlady** : the woman who owns a hotel, inn or apartment.

4 May

Just before I was about to take the coach, the landlady came up to my room.

'Must you go? Oh! young gentleman, must you go?'

Then she asked me, 'Do you know what day it is?' I told her that it was 4 May.

'No, no, more than that,' she said. 'It is the eve [2] of St George's Day. Don't you know that tonight at midnight all the evil [3] things in the world will have complete power?'

She then fell down on her knees and told me not to go, but I had to go.

The landlady then stood up, and taking a crucifix from her neck, offered it to me. I did not know what to do. I was a member of the Church of England, and we see such things as somewhat idolatrous. [4] But I did not want to offend the old lady.

She saw the doubt on my face and put the crucifix around my neck and said, 'Take it for your mother's sake.' [5]

I do not know why, but I am feeling worried. If this diary reaches Mina before I do, then it will be my good-bye. Here comes the coach!

5 May, the Castle

When I got on the coach the driver was talking with the landlady. Some people came and listened and then looked at me with pity. A number of words were repeated often. I looked them

---

2. **eve** : the night before.
3. **evil** : very bad, wicked.
4. **idolatrous** : considered divine. An idol is usually a sculpture that is considered a god.
5. **for your mother's sake** : for the good of your mother.

up in my polyglot [6] dictionary. They were 'Ordog' — Satan, 'pokol' — hell, 'stregoica' — witch, 'vrolok' and 'vlkoslak' — both of which mean the same thing, one being Slovak and the other Serbian for something that is either were-wolf [7] or vampire. (I must ask the Count about these superstitions.)

I soon forgot my fears as we travelled through this green hilly land of forests and farmhouses. The driver clearly wanted to arrive quickly to the Borgo Pass. [8] After some time we could see the Carpathian Mountains above these hills.

As it became dark, the other passengers kept telling the driver to go faster. Then through the darkness I could see an area of grey light ahead of us. Then the mountains seemed to come nearer to us on each side: we were entering the Borgo Pass. Then the coach stopped and we waited for the Count's coach to arrive. The driver said softly to another passenger that we were an hour early. Then he said to me, 'You see, no one is here for you. You can go on to Bukovina and then return another day.'

Just then the horses became very excited. The passengers screamed and crossed themselves. [9] A coach with four beautiful black horses arrived. Its driver was a tall man, with a long brown beard and a great black hat that hid his face. His eyes seemed red in the lamplight.

He said to our driver, 'You are early tonight, my friend.'

'The English gentleman was in a hurry,' our driver said.

---

6. **polyglot** : multilingual, with many languages.
7. **were-wolf** : a man that is part wolf.
8. **Pass** : an opening in the mountains through which you can travel.
9. **crossed themselves** : made the sign of the cross (in order to have the protection of Christ).

'That is why you told him to go on to Bukovina. You cannot deceive me, my friend. I know too much and my horses are too fast.' As this strange man spoke I could see his very red lips and his sharp teeth as white as ivory.

One of my companions in the coach whispered a line from a poem:

The dead travel fast.

The strange driver smiled at this and said, 'Give me the gentleman's luggage.' Then he put my bags into his coach quickly and helped me in with a hand that held me strongly. Without a word we drove into the darkness of the Borgo Pass. The coach went extremely fast, and it seemed to me that we were simply going around in a big circle, so I took note of some distinctive point. I then discovered that we were in fact going around in a circle. Then I looked at my watch and discovered that it was almost midnight.

Suddenly, on our left, I saw a blue flame. The driver stopped the horses and, jumping to the ground, disappeared into the darkness. Then the driver reappeared. I think I fell asleep and kept dreaming of this incident because it seemed to be repeated endlessly. Now it seems like an awful nightmare. 10

Once the flame appeared near the road and I could observe the driver making a strange construction of stones around it. Another time I saw the driver standing between me and the flame, and it seemed that I could still see it.

Then another time the driver stopped the coach and went even farther away. The horses began to tremble. 11 I could

10. **nightmare** : a very bad dream.
11. **tremble** : shake.

not understand why. But just then the moon came out from behind some black clouds and I saw around us a circle of wolves. All at once, with the appearance of the moon, they began to howl.

I shouted for the driver and tried to scare the wolves away. Then the driver appeared and shouted some command and waved his arms. The wolves moved away. This was so strange that I became too afraid to move or speak. Then we travelled for an endlessly long time. Suddenly, I saw that we had arrived in the courtyard of a large ruined castle.

5 May

I probably fell asleep because I did not notice our arrival at the Count's castle. When the coach stopped the driver jumped down and helped me out and then jumped back on the coach and drove away.

What was going to happen? What kind of people lived here? Was this the usual kind of thing that happened to a solicitor [12] who was sent out to explain the purchase [13] of a property in London to a foreigner?

Just then I heard the large door opening. Inside, stood a tall old man with a long white moustache and all dressed in black. The old man signalled with his right hand for me to enter, and said in excellent English with a strange accent, 'Welcome to my house! Enter freely and of your own will!' [14] He did not come

---

12. **solicitor** : lawyer, a person who prepares legal documents for buying land, etc.
13. **the purchase** : the buying, the acquisition.
14. **of your own will** : as you want.

closer to greet me, but stood like a statue. But the moment I entered, he moved forward and shook my hand so hard that it hurt. His hand felt more like the hand of a dead man than that of a living man. 'Welcome to my house,' he continued, 'Come freely. Go safely, and leave something of the happiness you bring.'

The strength of his handshake reminded me of the driver, so I said, 'Count Dracula?'

'I am Dracula,' he replied. 'Welcome, Mr Harker. Come in. You must eat and rest.'

He himself carried my bags up the stairs to a small room without windows and then into a great bedroom well lighted and warmed with a big fire.

I then washed and changed quickly because I was very hungry. When I went to the other room the Count said, 'Please be seated and eat as you please. Please excuse me if I do not join you, but I have already eaten.'

After dinner, I smoked a cigar and observed his face. His nose had peculiar nostrils. [15] His eyebrows were large and almost met over the nose. The mouth under the heavy white moustache had peculiarly sharp teeth, which went over the lips. His lips seemed incredibly red for a man of his age. His ears were pale and at the tops extremely pointed. The chin was broad and strong. His hands were broad with short fingers. Strange to say, there were hairs in the centre of the palms. [16] The nails were long and fine, and cut to a sharp point. In addition his breath stank [17] which gave me a feeling of nausea.

---

15. **nostrils** :

16. **palms** :

17. **stank** : (stink, stank, stunk) had a bad odour.

7 May

After breakfast I found a kind of a library. It was filled with books about England. While I was reading the Count came in and greeted me.

'I am glad you found my library. Unfortunately, I only know your language through books. I hope you can teach me how to speak it.'

'But, Count,' I said, 'you know and speak English very well.'

'Thank you,' he replied, 'but I only know the words and grammar, I don't know how to speak them. Everybody in London would know that I am a stranger. Here I am noble, but a stranger in a strange land is no one.'

I told him that I would be happy to teach him and then I asked if I could come into the library when I wanted.

'Yes, certainly,' he answered. 'You may go anywhere you wish in the castle, except where the doors are locked, where of course you will not wish to go. We are in Transylvania and Transylvania is not England.'

This led to much conversation. I asked him about the blue flames. He said that it was believed that on certain nights of the year when all the evil spirits have complete power — the night before in fact — those blue flames appear over places where treasure has been buried. Foreign armies had invaded this region many times and each time the residents buried their treasures to hide them from the invaders.

Then the Count and I looked at all the papers regarding the house and he signed the necessary documents. He then asked me how I had found such a good place. I showed him some photographs and read the notes I had taken. This very old property is called Carfax and its house is large. One large house nearby has recently become a lunatic asylum. [18]

---

18. **lunatic asylum** : a hospital where people with severe mental problems live.

The Dead Travel Fast

8 May

I began to fear that I wrote too much in this diary, but now I am glad that I did. I need these facts so that my imagination does not get out of control.

This morning I got up and hung my shaving mirror by the window. I began to shave when suddenly I felt a hand on my shoulder, and heard the Count's voice saying to me, 'Good morning.' I jumped because I was surprised that I had not seen his reflection in my mirror. In jumping, I cut myself slightly. I said good morning to the Count and looked at the mirror again to see if I had been mistaken. Now the Count was near me and still I could not see him in the mirror. In that moment I could see that the cut was bleeding a little. When the Count saw my face, his face showed a horrible anger, and he tried to grab my throat. I pulled away and his hand touched the crucifix around my neck. It made an instant change in him. The anger went away so quickly that it was difficult to believe that it had ever been there. 'Take care,' he said, 'take care how you cut yourself. It is more dangerous than you think in this country.' Then he grabbed my shaving mirror and said, 'And this is the horrible thing, this toy of man's vanity, that has caused this trouble.' Then he pulled open the window and threw it out.

Afterwards, I went down to have breakfast, but the Count was nowhere around. It is strange that I haven't seen him eat or drink yet. Then I went to look around the castle. I looked south from the window. The castle is on a precipice a thousand feet high! Doors, doors, doors everywhere and all locked. The only exit from the castle is from the windows.

The castle is a veritable prison, and I am a prisoner!

The text and **beyond**

FCE ❶ Comprehension check

For questions 1-7, choose the best answer — A, B, C or D.

1 Jonathan saw the crucifix as something that could
   A ☐ only protect Transylvanians.
   B ☐ not really protect anybody.
   C ☐ only protect sons.
   D ☐ only protect women.

2 What didn't the Count and his driver have in common?
   A ☐ a large beard
   B ☐ sharp white teeth
   C ☐ very strong hands
   D ☐ red lips

3 The voyage to the castle seemed like a bad dream because
   A ☐ wolves came near the coach and howled.
   B ☐ the driver did not talk.
   C ☐ the horses were beautiful, black and very fast.
   D ☐ the same strange events happened again and again.

4 The Count wanted Jonathan's help in purchasing the property and
   A ☐ learning English grammar correctly.
   B ☐ becoming like an English nobleman.
   C ☐ transporting his possessions to England.
   D ☐ speaking English like an Englishman.

5 People in Transylvania had often put their treasures underground
   A ☐ to keep them away from witches and vampires.
   B ☐ to give the dead money.
   C ☐ to keep them away from nobility like the Count.
   D ☐ to keep them away from foreign armies.

6   In the end, Jonathan was glad he had written so much in his diary
    because
    A [ ] it would help him to explain things to Mina.
    B [ ] writing helped him to relax and stay calm.
    C [ ] it kept him in touch with reality.
    D [ ] it helped him remember questions for the Count.

7   How was the Count supernatural?
    A [ ] He hated mirrors.
    B [ ] Blood excited him.
    C [ ] His breath stank.
    D [ ] He had no reflection.

2 The dead travel fast

The line 'the dead travel fast' comes from the narrative poem *Lenore*
by Gottfried August Bürger (1748-94). What do you think its meaning
is? Give reasons for your answer.

A [ ] The dead always have the best horses and carriages.
B [ ] The dead no longer have bodies and so they have no physical
      limits.
C [ ] Other ....

T: GRADE 7

3 Speaking: national customs

Prepare a short oral report about customs or beliefs in your country
to present to the class.

• Describe two supersitions or local customs.
• Say whether you believe in them or not.
• Say why people believe in superstitions.

4 Discussion

Bram Stoker got much of his information on Romanian superstitions from an essay called *Transylvanian Superstitions* (1885) by the British author Emily Gerard. She was married to a Hungarian officer, and lived for two years in Romania. She wrote that Transylvania could be called 'the land of superstition', in part because it was isolated from modern Europe and so old beliefs survived, and in part because several different cultures existed there.

Superstitions still exist in the modern world. Each country has its own. Who doesn't know that the number after 12 brings bad luck. But many don't know that the number after 3 brings bad luck in China, Japan and Korea.

Below are some superstitions from different countries. To see what these superstitions are, with your partner match the phrases in column A with those in column B. Report your answers to the class. Does everybody agree?

A

1 ☐ Turkey: If you stand between two people whose names are the same,

2 ☐ Argentina: If you find money — even a one-cent coin,

3 ☐ Italy: If somebody touches your feet with a broom while sweeping,

4 ☐ United States: If you spill salt,

5 ☐ Russia: If you give somebody knives as a gift,

B

A that person should give you a small amount of money.

B you should take a pinch of it and throw it over your left shoulder 'right into the eye of the devil'.

C then you will never get married.

D you should wish for something because your wish will come true.

E you will later receive money.

INTERNET PROJECT

When *Dracula* first appeared in 1897, wolves had a bad reputation in Britain and Europe. In fairy tales, *Little Red Riding Hood*, for example, wolves often represent evil. In real life, they were mostly feared. Now, things have changed considerably. Thanks to certain films like *Dances with Wolves* (1990), nature documentaries and numerous wolf organizations, wolves are now often admired. To find out more about these fascinating animals connect to the Internet and go to www.blackcat-cideb.com or www.cideb.it. Insert the title or part of the title of the book into our search engine. Open the page for *Dracula*. Click on the Internet project link. Go down the page until you find the title of this book and click on the relevant link for this project. Work with your partner and prepare a short report about wolves. Include some general information about them:

▶ where they live
▶ how big they are
▶ how they hunt.

You can also download some pictures and play some recordings of wolves howling.

Before you read

1 Vocabulary

Match the pictures (A-F) to the words (1-6). You can use a dictionary to help you.

1 drop	4 lizard
2 lid	5 shovel
3 graveyard	6 moonlight

2 Reading pictures

Look at the picture on page 29 and discuss these questions.

1 What is the Count doing? Why?
2 What would you compare the Count to in this picture?

CHAPTER **TWO**

A Prisoner in Count Dracula's Castle

 www.blackcat-cideb.com

12 May

Let me begin with facts, just facts.

Tonight the Count said, 'Have you written your first letter to your employer Mr Peter Hawkins?'

I replied that I had not.

'Then write now, my friend,' said the Count, 'and tell him you will stay here for another month.'

'Do you wish me to stay for so long?' I asked.

'I desire it much, and I will not accept your refusal. Your employer sent you here to do what I needed.'

I could see that I was in his power completely.

'Please, my good young friend,' continued the Count, 'when you write, write only about business.'

After I had written my letters, the Count took them and left the room. When he returned he told me to forgive him, but he had work to do and could not stay with me that evening.

Then he added, 'My dear young friend, if you leave your room, never fall asleep in other parts of the castle because you will not be safe.'

Later

When he left me I went to my room. Then, not hearing a sound, I came out and went up the stone stairs to where I could look out towards the south. It gave me a feeling of freedom to look out of the window. The beautiful view gave me peace. Then below me I saw something moving. It was the Count's head coming out of the window. At first I liked watching — it is incredible how small things become interesting when you are a prisoner. But my feelings changed to disgust and terror when I saw the whole man slowly come out from the window and begin to crawl down the castle wall face down. At first I could not believe my eyes, but it was true. The Count was climbing down the wall quickly like a lizard!

15 May

Once more I have seen the Count go down the high wall like a <u>lizard.</u> I knew he had left the castle so I decided to explore. I found many doors locked but finally I was able to push open one large door. I entered a part of the castle that was evidently where the noble ladies lived a long time ago.

Later: the morning of 16 May

When I finished writing in my diary, I felt sleepy. I remembered the Count's warning, but took pleasure in

disobeying him. I lay down on a couch and looked out of the window at the beautiful view. The soft moonlight was peaceful. I suppose I fell asleep. I hope so, but I am afraid that everything that happened was very real.

The room was the same, but I could see three young women. I thought I was dreaming because they didn't make shadows in the moonlight. They came close to me, and looked at me for some time, and then whispered. Two of them had dark hair. Their eyes appeared to be almost red. The other one had blonde hair and eyes like pale sapphires. [1] All three had brilliant white teeth that shone like pearls against the red of their voluptuous [2] lips. There was something that made me nervous, some desire and at the same time some horrible fear. I felt an evil, burning desire: I wanted them to kiss me with their red lips.

They whispered together and then they laughed an inhuman [3] musical laugh. The blonde one shook her head seductively, and one of the other two said, 'Go on! You are first and then we will follow.' Then the other one said, 'He is young and strong; there are kisses for us all.'

I lay quietly looking with my eyes half-closed at them in delightful anticipation. The fair girl came close and bent over me until I could feel her breath. It was very sweet, but it was also unpleasant, like blood.

The girls were then above and were about to bite me with their bright white teeth. Strangely, I did not feel fear but a strange pleasure.

---

1. **sapphires** : blue precious stones.
2. **voluptuous** : sensuous.
3. **inhuman** : not human, like some kind of demon.

A Prisoner in Count Dracula's Castle

Just then I had another sensation. I was conscious of the presence of the Count and of his great fury. I saw his strong hand grab the neck of the fair woman and pull her away. Her eyes shone with anger and her cheeks were red with passion. But the Count! I had never imagined such anger, not even in hell! He threw the woman back, and signalled to the others, just as he had done with the wolves. Then in a low powerful voice like a whisper he said, 'Do not touch him! Move back! This man belongs to me!'

The fair girl said to the Count, 'You never loved. You never love!' Then all three women laughed horribly.

'Yes, I can love,' replied the Count. 'You know that from the past. Now, I promise you that when I have finished with him you can kiss him as much as you want. Now, go! I must wake him up. I have work to do.'

'Isn't there anything for us tonight,' one of the women said, and pointed to a bag the Count had thrown on the floor. This bag moved as if there were something alive inside it. One of the women opened the bag. Then, if I heard correctly, there was the sound of a half-suffocated child. All three women were then around the bag, and then they disappeared into the moonlight.

Then the horror was too much for me, and I fainted.

19 May

Last night the Count asked me to write three letters. One letter says that I have almost finished my work here and am leaving in a few days. The next letter says that I am leaving the next day. The third letter says I left the castle and have arrived in Bistritz. The Count explained to me that these letters will

assure [4] my friends. I do not want to send these letters but there is nothing I can do. I asked the Count what dates I should put on the letters. He said, 'The first should be June 12, the second June 19 and the third June 29.'

I know now how long I have to live. God help me!

17 June

This morning, I heard some wagons arrive below. I looked out of the window and saw two large wagons pulled by eight big horses each. I ran to my door and discovered it was locked. Then I saw some Slovaks take large empty boxes off the wagons.

24 June, before morning

Last night, I saw the Count come out of the window. He was wearing my suit! And he was carrying that terrible bag the three women had taken away. Now I know what his plan is. He will post my letters, and any terrible thing he does in the town, the people will think I did it.

After a couple of hours I heard a woman screaming below. I ran to the window and saw a woman. Her hair was messy [5] and she held her hand over her heart. 'Monster, give me my child!' she shouted.

Somewhere above me I heard the hard metallic whisper of the Count. It was answered by the howling of wolves. Soon there were hundreds of wolves.

Then the woman stopped shouting, and the wolves left licking their lips.

---

4. **assure** : cause my friends to believe that I am fine.
5. **messy** : not in order, untidy.

A Prisoner in Count Dracula's Castle

25 June, morning

Last night one of my letters was posted. I must think. Action!

Horrible things only happen at night. I have not seen the Count during the day. Maybe he sleeps when everyone else is awake, and he is awake when everyone else is asleep. I must get into his room. But how?

I know! If the Count's body can crawl out of his window, I can crawl to his window. It will be dangerous, but I must do it. Good-bye Mina!

Same day, later

I have done it, and I have returned safely to my room. I must describe what happened. The stones of the castle are large, so I could hold on and climb to the window outside the Count's room. I opened the window and went in. I then went down a spiral stairway. [6] At the bottom there was a long tunnel that led to a chapel, which was once a graveyard. The ground had been recently dug and the earth had been placed in the large boxes brought in the wagons. Then I went into the vaults [7] of the chapel. In the first two I found nothing. In the third, however, I made a discovery.

There in one of the great boxes lay the Count! It was impossible to say whether he was alive or dead. His eyes were open but they were not like a dead man's eyes. His cheeks were warm and his lips were red. But there was no movement, no breath, no beating of the heart. I was certain he had the keys to

6. **spiral stairway:**

7. **vaults** : an underground room in a church in which the coffins containing dead bodies are put.

the castle, so I began to look in his pockets. But his eyes, even though they seemed dead, looked at me with such hate that I ran from the place back to his room. Then I climbed back to my room and tried to think...

29 June

Today is the date of the last letter I gave to the Count. I saw him crawl down from his window again like a lizard, and he was wearing my clothes. I went back to the library and fell asleep.

Later the Count woke me up and said, 'Tomorrow, my friend, you will return to England.'

'Why can't I go tonight?' I asked him.

'Because, dear sir, my driver and horses are away.'

'But I would walk with pleasure. I want to go now.'

He smiled a soft, evil smile and said, 'And your baggage?'

'I do not care about it. You can send it later.'

'Come, my dear young friend,' replied the Count. 'I do not want to hold you here, even though I am sad that you are going.'

I followed the Count down the stairs to the front entrance of the castle.

'Listen!' he said.

Nearby was the howling of wolves. He opened the door, which, to my surprise, was then unlocked. Outside the door were the wolves. I could do nothing. The Count had won. Now I knew how I was going to die.

'Shut the door. I will wait until morning!' I shouted. With one movement of his arm, the Count threw the door shut.

Silently we returned to the library, and after a minute I returned to my room. The last time I saw the Count, he was kissing his hand to me.

A Prisoner in Count Dracula's Castle

30 June, morning

These may be the last words I write in this diary. I slept until just before dawn. Then it became light, and I felt I was safe. I ran down to the entrance of the castle because I knew it was open. I tried to open the door, but the Count had locked it again. I had to have the key! I went back to the window again and decided to climb again to the Count's room. When I reached the Count's room it was empty. I could not find the key anywhere. I went through the door in the corner and down the winding stairway and along the tunnel. I knew where to find the monster.

The great box was in the same place, but the lid was on it. I lifted the lid and saw something which filled me with horror. There was the Count, but he looked younger. His white hair and moustache were now dark grey. His cheeks and white skin were red underneath. His lips were redder than before and on his mouth were blood drops that ran over his chin and neck. His body was full of blood. He was disgusting but I had to look for the key. I felt his whole body but I could not find the key. Then I stopped and looked at the Count. He had a terrible smile on his face. This was the horrible creature that I was helping to bring to London. Among the millions of people of London there would be enough blood forever. He would be able to create more and more demons like himself. This thought made me crazy. I picked up a shovel and tried to hit his horrible face, but just then he turned and looked at me. Some magical power of his eyes blocked my arm and I only cut his forehead. The shovel fell from my hand.

Then I heard the singing of the men who had come to take away the boxes. I ran up to the Count's room. When I arrived there, I waited. When the men entered the vault I would run

down and escape through the open door. I heard them open the door to the chapel. I started to run toward the door of the Count's room, but just then some wind blew the door shut. I was a prisoner again.

As I write this I can hear the men working below. They are carrying away the box with the Count and the other boxes filled with earth. Now I can hear the wagons going away with the boxes.

I am alone in the castle with those horrible women. No, Mina is a woman. These are devils.

I will not remain alone with them. I will try to climb down the castle wall farther than I tried before. I will take some gold with me. It could be useful later. I may find some way to leave this horrible place.

And then away for home! Away to the quickest and nearest train! Away from this terrible spot, from this terrible land, where the devil and his children still walk with the feet of humans!

I would rather die and be with God than to stay with these monsters. The precipice is very high, and if I fall and die, at least I will rest as a man.

Goodbye, all! Mina!

The text and **beyond**

1 Comprehension check
Answer the following questions.

1 How did Jonathan's feelings change as he watched the Count come out of the window?

2 Why did Jonathan decide not to listen to the Count's warning?

3 What were the three young women like?

4 What were they going to do to Jonathan?

5 Why did they stop?

6 What did the Count do to show that he could love?

7 How did Jonathan know when he was going to die?

8 What did the drivers take away from the castle?

9 What was the Count like when Jonathan found him in the chapel the first time?

10 What was the Count like when Jonathan found him in the chapel the second time?

11 Why did Jonathan hit the Count with a shovel?

12 In what ways did the Count keep Jonathan trapped in the castle?

13 Why were the people in the village going to think that Jonathan was evil?

14 How did Jonathan plan to escape?

'There was a long tunnel that led to a chapel, which was once a graveyard.'

Non-defining relative clauses add extra information to a sentence, but they are not essential to its meaning.

Defining clauses are essential to the meaning of a sentence: they tell us which person or thing we are talking about. In other words, if you take away a defining clause, the sentence no longer has any meaning or has a different meaning.

Non-defining clauses are separated from the rest of the sentences with commas.
Remember, too, that we use **who** for people and **which** for things.
Look at these examples:

Defining clauses

*This is the crucifix **which the landlady gave me**.*
*Jonathan Harker is the solicitor **who is now in Transylvania**.*

Non-defining clauses

*The crucifix, **which the landlady had given Jonathan**, stopped the Count from attacking Jonathan.*
*Jonathan Harker, **who works for Mr Hawkins**, is my guest at the castle.*

2 Non-defining relative clauses

Join the sentences in column A with those in column B using non-defining clauses with either 'who' or 'which'. The sentences should be true. There is an example at the beginning (0).

A

0 A friendly old woman gave Jonathan a crucifix.
A friendly old woman, who was the landlady of the Golden Krone Hotel, gave Jonathan a crucifix.

1 Jonathan left for the Count's castle on 4 May.

....

2 The Count's coach arrived.

....

3 One of Jonathan's companions on the coach said, 'The dead travel fast.'

....

4 The Count's breath had a terrible odour.

....

5 The Count was going to buy a property called Carfax.

....

6   Jonathan discovered he was a prisoner in the castle.

....

7   The Count knew English very well.

....

B

A   This made Jonathan feel sick.

B   This is a line from a famous German poem.

C   He could climb down walls like a lizard.

D   It was on a 1000-foot-high precipice.

E   It was pulled by four splendid horses.

F   ~~She was the landlady of the Golden Krone Hotel.~~

G   It was near a lunatic asylum.

H   It was the eve of St George's Day.

3 Writing

In the novel *Dracula* all the main characters have a chance to speak in the first person in their various letters and diaries. Well, almost everyone because the Count himself never does. His conversation is briefly reported by Jonathan. So, pretend that you are the Count and that you have a diary in English.

Write a diary entry of 120-180 words about Jonathan. Include this information:

- your first impression of Jonathan
- why you want to go to London
- how you stopped Jonathan from killing you
- how you plan to kill him.

You must invent some things. Make sure what you invent reflects the story. You can begin like this:

May 5

Finally, Jonathan Harker has arrived! I have been waiting for this day for years...

Real Vampires

In the early 1700s Europe experienced a vampire mania. All the newspapers of the age talked about them. A respected Biblical scholar named Dom Augustin Calmet (1672-1757) published an enormous book on vampires in 1746, and even though he did not exactly say that they really existed, he did not exactly say that they didn't exist either. The famous philosopher Voltaire (1694-1778) referred to them ironically. The great French biologist Comte de Buffon (1707-88) called a South American bat a 'vampire bat'. Then the Swiss philosopher Jean-Jacques Rousseau (1712-78) even wrote that there was every kind of proof to show that vampires really existed – there were government reports, church reports, legal documents and medical reports about vampires. And the really strange thing is, Rousseau was right – there really were hundreds of official reports of all kinds talking about vampires. For example, in 1731 Johannes Fluchinger, a medical officer of the Austrian army, was sent to investigate a case of vampires in the village of Medvegia in Serbia. In his report he wrote:

'I carried out the investigation with the assistance of two other doctors and a captain of the local infantry unit. They told me that a local soldier named Arnold Paole had said several times that a vampire had bitten him in Serbian Turkey. To free himself from the effect of the vampire he had eaten some of the earth from the vampire's grave and washed himself with its blood. Then, twenty days after Arnold Paole's death, various people said that he had come back from the grave to torment them, and four of these people actually died. So, following the advice of a local government official,

Lon Chaney as a vampire in the 1943 film **Son of Dracula**,
directed by Robert Siodmak.

who was an expert in vampires, the villagers dug up Paole forty
days after his death. They found his body intact. Fresh blood came
from his eyes, nose, ears and mouth. His shirt, shroud [1] and the
coffin were all filled with blood. The nails of the hands and feet had
fallen off with the old skin, but new skin and nails had grown in
their place.

1. **shroud** : a cloth used for wrapping a dead body.

From this they deduced that Arnold Paole was a vampire. According to the local custom, a stake was driven into his heart and in that moment he made a sad, low sound, and blood spurted forth from his body. The same day the body was burned to ashes. But that was not the end because one night a girl named Stanacka woke up at midnight screaming. She said that a man named Milloe, who had died nine weeks earlier, had attacked her. Three days later, the girl died. So some soldiers of Medvegia and I entered the cemetery and all the suspicious graves were opened and the bodies exposed. To the horror and wonder of everybody, almost all the bodies were perfectly preserved and had fresh blood on their faces, and they were fatter and redder than usual. So, we cut off their heads and then burned the bodies.'

These and similar reports by the highly respected Austrian army created a big sensation. In a certain sense, they still do because many books and Internet sites talk about these reports as proof of the existence of vampires. This is, of course, ridiculous, but the truth is much more fascinating.

First we should notice that a belief in vampires was certainly real, but it was only in the early 1700s that the major capitals of Europe began to learn about it. This was because Austria added parts of present-day Serbia and Romania to its empire in 1718. After this, Austrian officials began to hear about the strange local custom of digging up dead bodies and 'killing' them.

Actually, a belief in vampires had always existed there, and similar beliefs have always existed in different forms all over the world. A belief in vampires existed before people knew about the real causes of death and disease. They saw epidemics as personal events, and

Gary Oldman as
Count Dracula
in the 1992
film version
of **Dracula**
directed by
Francis Ford
Coppola.

they blamed the dead for death. So, the first person to die in an epidemic was then blamed for causing the epidemic that followed. It is impossible for us to imagine the terror people felt when, for some unknown reason, people began dying in great numbers. The folklorist Paul Barber wrote: 'Without any knowledge of physiology, pathology and immunology, how could people explain disease and death? The most common way was to blame death on the dead. They thought that the dead must be pacified and calmed and laid to rest correctly, and when nothing else worked, they killed the dead a second time.'

Then, as in the report quoted above, the villagers often dug up the grave of the dead person they thought was killing other people (or, in other words, the vampire). Then, they found a body much different from a living body. But they did not attribute these changes to decomposition as we would today. They saw them as proof that the body in the grave was the body of a vampire.

Any medical examiner today would tell you that Johannes Fluchinger's description of the vampire is a perfect description of a decomposing body. Again, we must remember that people once had much different ideas about death. They did not see the decomposing body as dead: they saw it as still dying. The process of dying was not as simple as we now see it: for them dying was a slow process of change from the world of the living to the world of the dead.

Of course, the huge interest in Vienna, Paris, London and the other important European cities in this strange belief from the wild parts of Europe eventually inspired writers. The first vampire poems appeared in German in the 1730s. The word 'vampire' entered the English language in 1734. These literary vampires had less and less to do with the vampires of folklore. In the end, literary vampires became tall, thin, pale and aristocratic. But the typical vampire of East European folklore was a robust, reddish-coloured peasant. Many other subconscious fears began to be associated with vampires. In short, Count Dracula and all his descendants in books and films have very little in common with the ones villagers and peasants of Transylvania looked for in their local graveyards.

1 Comprehension check

Say whether the following statements are true (T) or false (F), and then correct the false ones.

		T	F
1	In the early 1700s there was a veritable vampire mania in the big cities of Europe.	☐	☐
2	The Europeans did not take much interest in the stories of vampires coming from the East.	☐	☐
3	The Swiss philosopher Rousseau did not think there were any good reasons to believe in vampires.	☐	☐
4	The Austrian government did not take very seriously the various beliefs in vampires.	☐	☐
5	A belief in vampires was limited to Eastern Europe.	☐	☐
6	Fluchinger's description of Arnold Paole's dead body is still difficult for scientists to explain.	☐	☐
7	People used to think that the first person who died of a contagious disease was responsible for the deaths that followed.	☐	☐
8	People once thought that the decomposing body was, in a certain sense, still dying.	☐	☐
9	The first poems about vampires were written in English.	☐	☐
10	Dracula was the first literary vampire.	☐	☐
11	The vampires of books, poems and films have very little in common with the vampires of folklore.	☐	☐

Before you read

1 Vocabulary

Match the pictures (A-F) to the words (1-6). You can use a dictionary to help you.

1 sparrow	3 searchlight	5 safety pin
2 feather	4 helm	6 shawl

2 Listening

Listen to the first part of Chapter Three. You will hear about Mina Murray's friend Lucy Westenra and the three men who love her. For questions 1-5, complete the sentences.

1 Mina knows that Jonathan is doing fine because ....

2 Mina says that she has received .... letters from Lucy for a long time.

3 Lucy though that .... would be a good husband for Mina if Mina were not engaged to Arthur.

4 Quincey has travelled to .... places.

5 Mina's favourite part of Whitby is ....

The Count Arrives in England

Letter from Miss Mina Murray to Miss Lucy Westenra

9 May

My dearest Lucy,

Forgive me if I haven't written to you for such a long time, but I have had a lot of work. I can't wait to be with you[1] by the sea.

Jonathan has written me a few lines from Transylvania. He is well, and will return in about a week.

Tell me all the news when you write. You have not told me anything for a long time. I hear rumours[2] about a tall, handsome man?

Love,

Mina

1. **I can't wait to be with you** : I really want to be with you a lot.
2. **rumours** : news about something or someone transmitted by talking, but we don't know if it is true or false.

Letter from Lucy Westenra to Mina Murray

Wednesday

My dearest Mina,

Don't say I haven't written to you! I have already written you twice since we parted. Mr Arthur Holmwood is the handsome man that you have heard about. He often comes to see Mamma and me.

Some time ago, Arthur introduced me to a man who would be perfect for you, if you were not already engaged with Jonathan. His name is Dr Seward and he is only twenty-nine. He directs an immense lunatic asylum. He is very calm and very strong.

Mina, we have told all our secrets to each other since we were children. I love Arthur.

Write to me soon.

Lucy

Letter from Lucy Westenra to Mina Murray

24 May

My dearest Mina,

Thanks, and thanks, and thanks again for your sweet letter. It was so nice to be able to tell you about Arthur.

Mina, you will not believe it. I have never had a serious proposal of marriage until today. And today I have had three! You must not tell anyone except Jonathan. The first one I have already told you about. His name is Dr John Seward, the lunatic-asylum man. He was very cool on the outside, but very nervous. Unfortunately I had to say no. He asked me if there was someone else because he wanted to know if he had a chance. I told him there was. I felt so sad for him.

Evening.

Arthur has just gone, so I am feeling better, and I can tell you about number two. He is such a nice fellow. His name is Quincey P. Morris. He is a happy and friendly man, who has had fabulous adventures all around the world. Sometimes he even speaks American slang with me. Oh, Lucy, you must think me such a horrid flirt! He also asked me to marry him and I had to tell him no. Oh, about number three, Arthur. It was all so confused. It seemed only a moment after he entered the room when he had his arms around me and was kissing me. I am very happy.

Ever your loving,

Lucy

Mina Murray's Diary

24 July, Whitby

Lucy met me at the station. This is a lovely place. Between the abbey and the town is another church with a big graveyard full of tombstones. This is the nicest spot. There is a wonderful view of the town and the harbour. I will come here often. In fact, I am writing there now.

Dr Seward's Diary

5 June

To forget Mina I am studying a strange man named Renfield. His case grows more interesting the more I understand the man. He seems to have some secret plan. The good thing about Renfield is his great love for animals, but his pets are often strange. Now he is catching flies. He has a large quantity of them now. I tried to persuade him to get rid of [3] them. 'May I have three days. I will get rid of them then!' I told him yes.

18 June

Now he has spiders and he keeps feeding them with his flies.

1 July

His spiders are very numerous and are becoming a problem now. I told him that he must get rid of them too. He looked sad, but said yes. While I was talking to him, he disgusted me greatly. An enormous fly was flying around the room. He caught it and held it happily for a moment. Then he put it in his mouth and ate it.

19 July

We are progressing. Renfield now has many sparrows, and his flies and spiders are almost eliminated. When I came in he said he wanted to ask me for a big favour. I asked him what he wanted. He said, 'A kitten, a nice, little playful kitten that I can play with, and teach and feed and feed and feed!'

I was not surprised by this request, but I told him no.

20 July

I visited Renfield early in the morning. He was very happy and was placing sugar out to catch more flies. His sparrows were not there. He said that they had escaped. There were a few feathers around the room and on his pillow there was a drop of blood.

11 a.m.

The attendant has just been to me to say that Renfield has been very sick. He vomited a lot of feathers. 'I think, doctor,' he said, 'that he has eaten his birds!'

3. **get rid of** : eliminate, send away.

Cutting from The Dailygraph, *8 August*
(Pasted 4 *in Mina Murray's Diary)*

From a Correspondent

Whitby

Here in Whitby we have just had one of the greatest storms on record. The results of this storm were strange and unique.

Before the storm the weather had been very hot with no wind, which is not unusual for August. There were a lot of holidaymakers around. Then in the afternoon, the coastguard said that a storm was coming. The sunset was very beautiful. A little before ten o'clock in the evening the air grew very still and oppressive. Then the storm came with a rapidity that seemed incredible. All of nature was changed. The sea, which had been calm a moment before, was full of gigantic waves. In addition, a thick fog came.

A searchlight was used to help the boats come to shore in the fog. After a few minutes this searchlight discovered a ship that was coming into the port. Everybody was afraid that this ship would hit the rocks that were between the ship and the port. But just then even more fog came and covered everything. You could not see anything at all! Then, suddenly, the wind changed direction and blew away the fog. We could then see the ship moving quickly into the harbour. The searchlight continued to follow the ship and everyone then saw something horrible! There was a dead man tied to the helm of the ship, and his head went back and forth 5 with

4. **pasted** : attached with glue.
5. **back and forth** : from this side to that side, like the pendulum of a clock.

the movement of the ship. This ship had arrived safely in port, guided by the hand of a dead man!

The coastguard discovered that the name of the ship is *Demeter*. They also found the captain's log [6] that told of the ship's voyage from Varna on the coast of Romania to Whitby.

The log told about strange things that happened on the ship, and the presence of a strange man. One by one the crew died until only the captain was left. He tied himself to the wheel and held a crucifix in his hand. That is how we found him, except he was dead!

Mina Murray's Diary

11 August, 3 a.m.

Lucy sleepwalked [7] when she was younger and then she stopped, but now she has started again. Earlier this evening, I fell asleep as soon as I had closed my diary... Suddenly I woke up and felt very afraid. I looked around and saw that Lucy's bed was empty. I looked around the house and could not find her.

I found the front door open, so I went outside. I ran all the way to the West Cliff and looked across the harbour to the East Cliff, where Lucy and I like to sit.

It was far away but I could see well in the moonlight, and on our favourite seat I saw someone dressed in white and lying on the bench. I thought I saw something dark over the figure in white. I could not see whether it was a man or a beast because a cloud blocked the moon. I ran down the stairs of the West Cliff,

6. **log** : diary.
7. **sleepwalked** : walked when she was asleep; suffered from somnambulism.

through the town and up the stairs of the East Cliff to our favourite seat. When I was close, I could see something long and black bending over the white figure.

I called, 'Lucy! Lucy!' and something lifted its head and I could see a white face and red, shining eyes. I ran to the seat and found Lucy lying there, completely alone. She was still sleeping and breathing with difficulty. I put a shawl on her and closed it at her throat with a big safety pin. I think I pricked [8] her throat by accident with the safety pin because she put her hand on her throat. I then accompanied her home.

15 August

Lucy's mother has told me that she is dying. The doctor said that her heart is very weak. She must not be excited for any reason, or she will die. I must not tell her that Lucy has been sleepwalking again.

Letter about the delivery of 50 boxes of earth to Carfax Mansion from Samuel F. Billington & Son, Solicitors, to Carter, Paterson & Company, London

17 August

Dear Sirs,

Please deliver these fifty boxes to Carfax. You should place them in the old chapel of the mansion. We have enclosed the keys, because the owner of the mansion has not arrived yet.

Please deliver these boxes quickly.

Faithfully yours,

Samuel F. Billington & Son

---

8. **pricked** : punctured, made a small hole with a pin.

1 Comprehension check

Match the phrases in column A with those in column B to make true sentences. There are three phrases in column B that you do not need to use.

A

1. ☐ Mina didn't write to Lucy for a long time
2. ☐ Lucy was worried that Mina had a bad opinion of her
3. ☐ Mina liked going to the graveyard
4. ☐ There was a little blood on Renfield's pillow
5. ☐ The newspaper article called the storm strange
6. ☐ The captain did not fall down when he died
7. ☐ Mina thought that Lucy moaned
8. ☐ Mina was not surprised that Lucy sleepwalked to the East Cliff

B

A because she enjoyed the panorama from there.

B because she had pricked Lucy with the safety pin.

C because Lucy had sleepwalked as a child.

D because she had so many things to do.

E because three men wanted to marry her.

F because she had a nightmare.

G because he had tied himself to the helm.

H because she refused to marry Dr Seward.

I because he had eaten his sparrows.

J because she had been in Transylvania.

K because it arrived so quickly on a hot and calm day.

2 Crossword

Read the clues and complete the crossword.

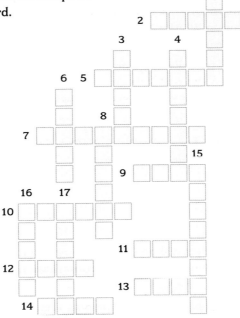

Across

2 Move using your hands and legs together.
5 Say something softly.
7 A bad dream.
9 Make a long, sad sound (used for wolves).
10 A piece of glass with a silver back in which you can see your image.
11 The document that says what you want to be done with your possessions when you are dead.
12 In a short time.
13 The opposite of 'living'.
14 The people who work on a ship or airplane.

Down

1 If something belongs to you, you are its...
3 Say something loudly.
4 A kind of bird.
6 Have a bad smell.
8 Terrible fear.
15 A woman who owns an inn, house or other property.
16 Disorderly, not in order.
17 Information passed from one person to another.

3 Writing

Pretend you are the Count and write a diary entry of 150-250 words about your departure from Transylvania, your arrival in England and your first days in Whitby. You can use facts from the book, but you will also have to use your imagination.

Include some of the following information:

- your feelings about your invasion of England
- how you brought the *Demeter* across the seas
- why you chose Lucy
- what you are planning to do now

T: GRADE 8

4 Speaking: health

Lucy the sleepwalker will be Dracula's first servant in England. Her problem with sleeping makes her vulnerable in some way to the vampire, to evil.

How are sleep and problems with sleeping seen today? Talk with your partner about the following points and then present your ideas to the class.

1 Talk about a film or book where people with sleeping problems or strange dreams are associated with the supernatural.
2 What was the strangest or the most frightening dream you have ever had?
3 Have you ever had problems sleeping?
4 Describe some tricks you know for falling asleep.

INTERNET PROJECT ◀◀◀

Bram Stoker set part of *Dracula* in the lovely seaside town of Whitby. To find out more about Whitby connect to the Internet and go to www.blackcat-cideb.com or www.cideb.it. Insert the title or part of the title of the book into our search engine. Open the page for *Dracula*. Click on the Internet project link. Go down the page until you find the title of this book and click on the relevant link for this project. Prepare a short report on Whitby:

▶ show pictures of the places mentioned in *Dracula*

▶ explain the origin of the story about the *Demeter*

▶ explain how the town pays tribute to Dracula

▶ explain why Whitby is a popular holiday spot.

Before you read

1 Prediction

Look at the title of Chapter Four. Why do you think it is called 'Giving and Taking Blood'? What do you think will happen in this part of the story?

2 Reading pictures

Look at the picture on page 65. Discuss the questions with your partner and then present your ideas to the class.

1   Who is the woman in the picture? Describe her.

2   What is strange about her?

3   What do you think has happened to her?

3 Listening

Listen to the first part of Chapter Four. For questions 1-7 complete the sentences.

1   Jonathan has been .... so he hasn't been able to send Mina any letters.

2   Mr Hawkins says Mina and Jonathan should ....

3   Jonathan and Mina will .... only if they really have to do it.

4   Professor Van Helsing is ....

5   Van Helsing thinks that Lucy could ....

6   Van Helsing goes back to ....

7   Lucy needs ....

Giving and Taking Blood

Mina Murray's Diary

19 August

Joy, joy, joy, although not all joy. At last news from Jonathan. He has been ill. That is why he hasn't written. He is in a hospital in Budapest. I am going there immediately to help him. Mr Hawkins thinks it would be a good idea, if we married there.

Dr Seward's Diary

19 August

Strange and sudden change in Renfield last night. Normally he is very nice and respectful with the attendant. But last night Renfield said to him, 'I don't want to talk to you. You are not important now. The Master is near. He is coming.'

Letter from Mina Harker to Lucy Westenra

Budapest, 24 August

My dearest Lucy,

I know you are anxious to hear all that has happened since we parted. I found Jonathan greatly changed. I am now writing at his bedside. He is waking!

When he woke he asked me for his coat. In his coat there was a notebook. He saw that I was interested in it. He told me that it contained all the secrets of what happened, but he said that now he does not want to know them. He said, 'I want to begin my life here with our marriage.' So we both agreed never to look at the notebook unless it was absolutely necessary. Yes, my dear Lucy, we are going to be married. After this talk Jonathan fell asleep again. I asked the nurse if we could be married this afternoon, and I am now waiting for her reply...

Jonathan woke up, and we were married. I am so happy. I hope you will be as happy as we are now!

Love,

Mina

Letter from Arthur Holmwood to Dr Seward

31 August

My dear Jack,

I want you to do me a favour. Lucy is ill. She has no special disease, but she looks terrible. I need your help. You must come and see her. I know it will be difficult for you, but you must do it for her. I want to talk to you alone after you have seen her. You must come!

Arthur

Giving and Taking Blood

Letter from Dr Seward to Arthur Holmwood

2 September

My dear old fellow,

I examined Lucy and since I am not able to understand her problem, I have written to my old friend and master, Professor Van Helsing of Amsterdam. He knows about every strange disease in the world. He is a philosopher and one of the most advanced scientists in the world. He also has an open mind, a lot of courage and the kindest heart in the world.

Yours always,

John Seward

Letter from Dr Seward to Arthur Holmwood

3 September

My dear Art,

Van Helsing has come and gone. He came with me to see Lucy when her poor, dying mother was out. He examined her carefully. Later when we were alone, he told me that Lucy's situation is very serious. It is a question of life or death. I asked him what he meant, but he said that he must think first. Don't be angry with me, Art. He will speak clearly when he has understood Lucy's situation. Now, Van Helsing must return to Amsterdam, but he will return.

Your friend,

Jack

Telegrams from Dr Seward to Professor Van Helsing, Amsterdam

4 September — Lucy is doing better today.

5 September — Lucy is still doing better. She has a good appetite and eats normally. Her colour is coming back.

6 September — Terrible change for the worse. Come at once!

Dr Seward's Diary
7 September

The first thing that Van Helsing said to me when we met was, 'Have you said anything to Arthur yet?'

'No,' I said, 'I wanted to wait until I saw you.'

'Good,' he replied, 'he should not know now. Perhaps, he will never know, but if it is necessary, he will know all.'

We went to Lucy's house. When we saw her, we were both shocked. She was terribly pale and the bones of her face were prominent. Van Helsing and I left the room.

'My God!' he said, 'this is horrible. We have no time to lose! She will die because she doesn't have enough blood. We must give her a transfusion.'

We then went downstairs to prepare the transfusion. Just then someone knocked at the front door. It was Arthur.

'Jack,' he said, 'I was so worried that I came immediately.'

'Sir,' said Van Helsing, 'Lucy needs blood immediately, or she will die. We are going to perform a blood transfusion to put the blood from your full veins into her empty veins.'

When we arrived in Lucy's room, Van Helsing gave Lucy a narcotic to make her sleep. When Van Helsing was certain she was sleeping, he called Arthur into the room.

'You can give her one little kiss now, while we prepare the instruments,' said Van Helsing.

Van Helsing performed the transfusion quickly and accurately. As the blood left Arthur and entered Lucy's veins, some life entered her face. Arthur, however, became paler and weaker.

64

When the transfusion was finished, Van Helsing said, 'I think this brave lover deserves another kiss.' He began to move Lucy's head on the pillow. As he did so, a narrow, black band that Lucy always wore around her neck moved. It showed a red mark on her throat. Arthur did not notice it, but I could see that Professor Van Helsing did.

'Now,' said the Professor, 'take Arthur down and give him some port wine and let him lie down to rest.'

When I returned, Van Helsing and I looked at the red mark again. We saw that there were two punctures over the external jugular vein. I thought that these two punctures were the cause of Lucy's loss of blood. But that was impossible. If blood had come out of those two punctures, Lucy's bed would be full of blood.

'I must go back to Amsterdam tonight,' Van Helsing said. 'There are some books and things I will need. You must remain here tonight with Lucy. You must watch her every second!'

8 September

I was awake all night watching Lucy. This morning she woke up much better.

This evening I went to Lucy's room again to keep her company during the night. She was happy that I was there. She seemed to be falling asleep, when she forced herself to wake up again. She did this two or three times.

'Don't you want to sleep?' I asked.

'No, I'm afraid,' she replied.

'Afraid to go to sleep? Why? Everybody likes sleeping,' I said.

'Not if you are like me. Sleep, for me, is the beginning of horror,' she said.

'The beginning of horror. What does that mean?' I asked.

Giving and Taking Blood

'I don't know. I don't know,' she said, 'and that is what makes it so horrible! A weakness comes to me when I am asleep.'

'But, my dear girl,' I said, 'you can sleep tonight. I am here watching you, and I promise you that nothing will happen.'

'Ah, I can trust you,' she said.

'I promise you that if I see that you are having a bad dream I will wake you at once,' I said.

'You will? Oh will you really wake me? You are very good to me. Then I will sleep!' And as soon as she had finished the sentence, she fell asleep.

9 September

'You are not going to stay awake tonight,' Lucy said to me. 'There is a nice room next to mine where you can sleep. If there is any problem, I will call you immediately. Tonight you must sleep.'

I was so tired that I accepted her offer and slept in the other room.

10 September

The Professor put his hand on my head, and I woke up immediately.

'And how is our patient,' he said.

'She was well when I left her, or rather when she left me,' I answered.

'Come, let us go and see,' he said. And we went to her room.

The blind [1] was down and the room was dark. I raised the blind and the room filled with light.

---

1. **blind** : piece of cloth over a window used to keep sunlight out of a room.

'My God!' said the Professor. His face became pale and he pointed at the bed.

There on the bed was poor Lucy. She appeared to have lost consciousness.

'Quick,' he said, 'We must give her another transfusion. And this time Arthur is not here, so you must give her your blood.'

11 September

This afternoon I went to Lucy's house and found the Professor very happy and Lucy much better. A moment after my arrival, a big package from abroad arrived for the Professor. He opened it and pulled out some white flowers.

'These are for you, Lucy,' he said.

'For me? Oh, Dr Van Helsing!'

While he was speaking, Lucy was looking at the flowers and smelling them. Then she threw them down and said, 'Oh, Professor, I think you are joking with me. These flowers are only common garlic.'

To my surprise, the Professor became angry and said, 'I never joke! Everything I do is serious. Do not try to block my work.'

Then he saw that he had frightened Lucy and he said quietly, 'Oh, Lucy, do not be afraid of me. I am doing this for your good.'

After we had finished, I said, 'Well Professor, I know you always have a reason, but I don't understand what you are doing. A sceptic would say that you are using magic to keep out an evil spirit.'

'Perhaps I am!' he answered quietly as he began to make the garlic necklace.

Giving and Taking Blood

Dr Seward's Diary

13 September

Van Helsing and I went to see Lucy. We arrived at eight o'clock. It was a beautiful morning. When we entered the house, Lucy's mother said to us, 'You will be happy to know that Lucy is better. She is still asleep now.'

Van Helsing smiled and said, 'My medicine is working!'

'Don't take all the credit, Professor,' said Mrs Westenra. 'I helped Lucy too.'

'What do you mean?' asked the Professor.

'Well,' she replied, 'last night she was sleeping well, but there was the terrible smell of those flowers, so I took them out and opened the window.' And then she left.

For the first time, I saw Van Helsing lose control of himself.

'God! God! God!' he said. 'What have we done to deserve this?'

Then we went and prepared ourselves for another transfusion. This time, Van Helsing himself gave blood.

Article from the newspaper The Pall Mall Gazette, *18 September*

The Escaped Wolf

I went to the Zoological Gardens to interview the keeper about the escaped wolf. He told me that the name of the escaped wolf was Bersirker. 'On the day the wolf escaped,' he said, 'there was a strange man in front of the wolf cage. He was a tall, thin man. He had red eyes. He said, 'These wolves are upset about something.' 'Maybe it's you,' I replied. 'No, they wouldn't hurt me,' he said and smiled, showing his sharp, white teeth. That night at around midnight I went to the cage and found the bars broken and the wolf gone. That is all I know.'

Lucy Westenra's Diary

17 September, night.

I went to bed with the flowers, and soon feel asleep.

Some flapping [2] at the window waked me. I was not afraid, but I wished Dr Seward was in the next room. Dr Van Helsing said that he had sent him a telegram telling him to come, but Dr Seward had not arrived. Outside I heard a strange howling. I went to the window and looked, but I could only see a big bat which was flapping against the window. I went back to bed, and then my mother came in. She said, 'I was worried about you.' She then got into bed with me.

The flapping against the window continued, and my mother was very afraid. Then the howling began again, and then there was a crash. The head of a giant wolf had broken through the window. My mother screamed in fright. For a second or two she pointed at the wolf and then she made strange, horrible sounds. Then she fell over dead on top of me. I continued looking at the window, but the wolf went away and lots of little specks [3] were blown in. I don't remember anything else for a few minutes.

The air seems full of specks turning around in circles. The lights are blue and dim. My dear mother is gone! And now I must go too. Good-bye, dear Arthur! God protect you, and God help me!

2. **flapping** : sound of moving wings.
3. **specks** : little particles.

The text and **beyond**

1 Comprehension check

Say whether the following statements are true (T) or false (F), and then correct the false ones.

		T	F
1	Renfield usually treated people badly.	☐	☐
2	Dr Seward called for Arthur when he realized Lucy's condition was serious.	☐	☐
3	Lucy's condition got better after the transfusion.	☐	☐
4	Arthur's condition got worse after the transfusion.	☐	☐
5	Dr Seward concluded that Lucy had lost blood through the punctures on her neck.	☐	☐
6	Lucy was afraid to sleep because she had bad dreams.	☐	☐
7	Lucy understood immediately that the flowers were not a gift.	☐	☐
8	Without the garlic flowers, Lucy got better.	☐	☐
9	The wolf jumped on Lucy's mother and killed her.	☐	☐
10	Lucy was certain that she was going to die.	☐	☐

2 Summary

Fill in each gap with a phrase to complete the summary of Chapters 1-4.

Jonathan Harker, a young solicitor, was going to the castle of his client, a local nobleman named Count Dracula.

The landlady of his hotel, though, told him not to go. It was the eve of St George's Day when (1) ....

Jonathan left anyway. At Borgo Pass he got on the coach sent by Count Dracula. His journey to the Count's castle seemed to him like (2) ....

The Count greeted Jonathan at the door of the castle. Jonathan soon noticed many strange things about the Count's appearance. For example the Count had (3) ....

At first, Jonathan thought that Count was a friendly aristocrat interested in learning more about (4) ....

But then one morning while he was shaving, the Count came up behind him. Strangely, though, the Count was not (5) .... Also, the Count became incredibly angry when (6) ....

Jonathan soon realized that he was prisoner, and that the Count was going to kill him. He also discovered the Count was a vampire. Once the Count was in London, he would have (7) ...., and he would also create (8) ....

Jonathan managed to escape, and the Count arrived on a ship at the town of Whitby. He did not wait to begin acting.

Mr Renfield, a patient in (9) .... next to the Count's new property, knew that the Count was near. The Count also began to (10) .... of Lucy Westenra. Lucy was the best friend of Jonathan's fiancée.

Lucy's fiancé soon noticed that there was something wrong with her. She was becoming (11) .... He asked his friend Dr Seward to examine her. Dr Seward came but he did not understand the problem so he called his teacher Dr Van Helsing. Van Helsing tried to save Lucy. First he used (12) .... and then, strangely, garlic flowers. In the end, these things could not stop her from getting worse and worse.

❸ Vocabulary

A **The words below all come from this chapter. Find their opposites in the box. There are four words in the box that you do not need to use.**

quickly	stupid	carelessly	bright	calm	dangerous
sadness	servant	cowardly	strength	rare	dull	far
relaxed	gradual	rude	angry	dark	old-fashioned

1 upset   ...calm...............
2 respectful   ....
3 advanced   ....
4 master   ....

5 anxious   ....

6 sudden   ....

7 joy   ....

8 pale   ....

9 accurately   ....

10 brave   ....

11 weakness   ....

12 common   ....

13 dim   ....

14 sharp   ....

15 near   ....

B Fill in the gaps in the sentences below with one of the words above or their opposites that you have just found.

1 Jonathan Harker, an ordinary London solicitor, turns out to be a very .... man who is willing to fight vampires.

2 When Jonathan was first coming to the Count's castle he saw .... blue lights.

3 The vampire's main .... is that it cannot move about during the day.

4 The Count made a .... movement away from Jonathan when he saw the crucifix.

5 Jonathan felt a deep .... when he thought that he was going to die in the Count's castle.

6 Renfield considered himself Count Dracula's loyal ....

7 Although vampires were an ancient danger, only a scientist with .... knowledge could defeat them.

8 Wolves are .... animals in London.

9 Dracula had .... teeth, just like a wolf.

10 Victims of vampires have .... faces because they have lost blood.

11 Dracula planned his invasion of England very ....

12 Rats and flies are .... in big cities.

FCE ④ Word formation

Read the text below. Use the word given in capitals at the end of some lines to form a word that fits in the space in the same line. There is an example at the beginning (0).

Blood transfusion

William Harvey (1578-1657) first described the
mechanism of blood (0) ..circulation..... . In truth, the   **CIRCULATE**
Syrian doctor Ibn al-Nafis (1213-88) should be given
credit for this discovery, but Europe did not know
about his work then. In any case, in 1667, Jean-
Baptiste Denis performed the first (1) ....   **RECORD**
transfusion — (2) ...., Denis's father was a   **INTERESTING**
hydraulic engineer.
Denis put sheep blood into a human. This sheep blood
was fairly (3) ...., but it wasn't very   **HARM**
helpful. It was not until 1818 that a (4) ....   **SUCCESS**
transfusion of human blood to another human was
performed by the (5) .... doctor James   **BRITAIN**
Blundell. Blundell also created many instruments for
doing transfusions. Still, most blood transfusions
were (6) .... until the Austrian   **SUCCESS**
(7) .... Landsteiner discovered blood types   **PATHOLOGY**
— A, B, O, AB — in 1901. Doctors finally knew that
people could only receive certain types of blood.
For example, someone with blood type A can only
receive blood type A or blood type O. If, however,
you receive the wrong blood type, it can easily be
(8) .... So, we can see that Lucy, who was   **DEAD**
very (9) .... to be bitten by a vampire in   **LUCK**
modern-day England, was very (10) .... to   **LUCK**
survive three blood transfusions before Karl
Landsteiner's discovery.

⑤ Discussion

What do you think the blood transfusions in this chapter show or symbolise? Discuss with other students.

Vampire Bats

A bat in flight.

Does a flapping of wings outside your window mean a vampire is near? Well, in Java there is a bat called the flying fox that has a wingspan of 1.7 metres and a body length of 42 centimetres. During the day it hangs upside-down from tree branches in groups of hundreds and thousands. When these bats finish their daytime rest and fly off into the night, it is a frightening spectacle, especially for those who have read *Dracula*. But there is really no reason to be afraid because these bats eat fruit, not blood.

Then there is a bat with large claws and big teeth, but this one eats fish. What about blood? Isn't there a bat that eats blood?

Well, among the more than 1,000 species of bats in the world, there are three that drink blood. They all live in the American tropics. They are a lot smaller than the flying foxes of Java, being only around 8 centimetres long. They are incredibly agile though, even when they are not flying. They can run on all four legs, or standing up on their back legs, and they jump very well too.

They feed on the blood of both birds and mammals, but they especially like to feed on domestic animals like cows, horses and goats.

Like most bats, vampire bats locate their pray using echolocation, or sonar; they emit acute sounds that bounce off objects around them and return to the bats as echoes. This sonar system of bats is so sophisticated that we can say that bats 'see acoustically'. When a vampire bat has located a sleeping cow, for example, it generally lands on the ground near the animal. Then with great agility it runs quickly and quietly towards the animal, and then jumps on it like a frog. It then looks for an area with little fur, like on the legs or around the ears. Vampire bats also have special cells in their noses that are used as infrared detectors – in this way they can find where the blood of an animal is closer to the surface. Then the vampire bites the animal with its razor-sharp teeth. This bite is almost painless and the sleeping animal is not

A bat hanging from a tree with wings wrapped around its body.

A vampire bat.

awakened. Once the animal is bitten, the blood comes out and the vampire bat licks it up. Also, there are special proteins in the bat's saliva which prevent blood from coagulating. Recent studies have shown that these proteins, which have been named 'draculin' after the famous fictional vampire, may be very useful in treating people who have had heart attacks and strokes.

But this is not all. These animals have other special adaptations for their blood-eating life. Once a vampire bat has consumed its meal of blood, it weighs 50% more than usual, and it is now too heavy to fly. However, after about 2 minutes a bat eliminates much of the liquid part of blood. Even now, though, the vampire weighs about 20% more than usual, and so vampire bats are the only bats that have the ability to jump up straight in the air and then fly. Another interesting adaptation of these fascinating little mammals is social. It is fairly common for vampire bats not to find food, and after two days without food they die. So vampire bats, which live in groups, often share their meals of blood with those that did not eat.

Vampire bats often bite people, especially those people who sleep outdoors. They generally bite people on the cheeks or toes. The vampire bite is not particularly dangerous in and of itself. People who have been bitten say that it feels like a razor cut when you are shaving. Still, there is the danger of getting rabies, a fatal viral infection. This is why vampire bats are dangerous and farmers try to destroy them, but without much luck. In fact, the increase in the number of domestic animals has surely helped vampire bats to increase their numbers. So, a flapping of wings at the window, at least in tropical America, may really mean a vampire is near.

1 Comprehension check
Answer the following questions.

1 What do flying foxes eat?
2 How many different kinds of bats are there in the world?
3 Where do vampire bats live?
4 How big are vampire bats?
5 How do vampire bats find their prey?
6 What do vampire bats use their infrared detectors for?
7 What is 'draculin'?
8 Why do vampire bats eliminate the liquid content of their meal of blood so quickly?
9 Why are vampire bats dangerous to people?

Before you read

1 Reading pictures

Look at the picture on page 83 and discuss the questions with your
partner. Present your ideas to the rest of the class.

1   What is happening in this picture?

2   What is Lucy about to do? Why?

3   What do you think will happen next?

Look at the picture on page 87 and discuss the questions with your
partner. Present your ideas to the rest of the class.

1   Who are the characters in the picture? Where are they?

2   What are they doing? Why?

3   What do you think is going to happen?

2 Listening

Listen to the first part of Chapter Five and answer the questions.

1   What did Van Helsing tell Dr Seward to do in his telegram?

2   When did he send the telegram?

3   When did it arrive?

4   What did Lucy tell Arthur to do when she woke up?

5   How did Arthur react when Van Helsing stopped him from kissing
Lucy?

6   What did Van Helsing promise Lucy that he would do?

The Bloofer Woman

Dr Seward's Diary

18 September

Dr Van Helsing and I arrived at Lucy's house. On 16 September Van Helsing had sent me a telegram in which he told me to spend the night protecting Lucy. I had only received the telegram this morning, so we were both worried since Lucy had spent the night alone! Nobody answered the door when we knocked. We opened the door and ran up to Lucy's room. How can I describe what we saw? Two women lay on the bed, Lucy and her mother. Her mother was covered with a white sheet, but her face was not covered. We could see a look of horror on it. She was dead, and Lucy looked dead too. The garlic flowers were not around her neck. They were now on her dead mother. The punctures on her neck looked horribly white and torn. The Professor bent over Lucy, and he listened. Then he jumped up, and cried out to me, 'It's not too late! Quick! Quick! Bring the brandy!'

We prepared ourselves for another blood transfusion.

20 September

I spent the whole night next to Lucy's bed. At six o'clock in the morning Van Helsing came in. When he saw Lucy's face, he said, 'Pull up the blinds! I need light!' Then he started to examine her carefully. When he looked at her neck, he shouted, 'My God! My God!' I came over to look too. The holes on her throat had absolutely disappeared.

'She is dying,' he said. 'She will soon be dead. Go and bring Arthur here.'

When Arthur and I came back to the room, Lucy said, 'Arthur! Oh my love, I am so happy you have come!' Arthur was going to kiss Lucy when Van Helsing said, 'No, not yet! Hold her hand — it will comfort her more.'

Arthur sat down next to her and held her hand. She fell asleep. Then she began to change. She breathed with difficulty and her mouth opened, and her teeth seemed longer and sharper. Then her eyes opened, but she was still asleep.

'Arthur,' she said in a strange voluptuous voice, 'I am so happy you have come! Kiss me!'

Just as Arthur was going to kiss Lucy, Van Helsing grabbed him and pushed him away. Arthur was so surprised that he did not move. I kept looking at Lucy and saw anger in her face and her sharp teeth closed with force.

A moment later, Lucy woke up again and took Van Helsing's hand in hers and kissed it. 'Thank you, my friend,' she said. 'Protect Arthur and give me peace.'

'I promise,' replied Van Helsing. Then he said to Arthur, 'Come, my child, take her hand in yours and kiss her on the forehead, and only once.'

Then Lucy's eyes closed and her breathing became difficult.

'It is all over,' said Van Helsing. 'She is dead.'

I took Arthur out of Lucy's room and downstairs. When I returned, I said to Van Helsing, 'Well, now the poor girl will have peace.'

'No,' replied Van Helsing, 'this is only the beginning.'

'What do you mean?' I asked. But his only answer was, 'We can do nothing now. We must wait and see.'

An article from The Westminister Gazette, *25 September*

A Hampstead Mystery

Numerous children have returned home late in the evening or have not been found until the next day. All the children have said that they did not return home because of the 'bloofer lady.' Now, many children pretend to be the 'bloofer lady.' It is very funny to see the little children playing this game.

But the situation is serious, because all the children who have disappeared have returned home with punctures on their necks. Perhaps a rat or a small dog made these punctures.

Letter from Van Helsing to Mrs Mina Harker

> *24 September*
> *Dear Madam,*
> *Please forgive me for writing, but Arthur Holmwood gave me permission to read all of Lucy's letters. I see that she and you were very good friends. May I come to Exeter to talk with you? I need your help to help other people. It is very important. Please do not tell your husband now. I do not want to upset him.*
> *Again please forgive me,*
> *Van Helsing*

Mina Harker's Diary
25 September

Van Helsing has come and gone. What a strange meeting! Everything is like a dream. I gave him my diary so he could read about what happened to Lucy. He was very grateful. Then he asked me about Jonathan. I told him that he had had a brain fever,[1] but that he was much better now. But then I had to ask him for help since Jonathan seemed afraid; we had seen a strange man in London who Jonathan said was Count Dracula. After this, I decided that I had to read Jonathan's diary.

'What I am going to tell you, Dr Van Helsing, is very, very strange,' I said.

'Oh, my dear,' he replied, 'if you only knew how strange this story is.'

I then gave him Jonathan's diary too. He said he will read it immediately.

---

1. **brain fever** : illness of the brain that caused him to have a high temperature.

The Bloofer Woman

Dr Seward's Diary

26 September

Well, there is no end to this story. A week ago, I thought everything was finished.

But now I am beginning again. Until this afternoon, I had no reason to think about Lucy.

Renfield has been collecting his flies and now he has started with the spiders, so he has not caused me any trouble.

I had a letter from Arthur, written on Sunday. He is doing well, considering his loss.

Quincey Morris is with him, and that is a great help — Quincey is such an enthusiastic and energetic person.

Quincey wrote me a short letter too. He says that Arthur is beginning to recover.

So, I do not need to worry about them.

As for me, I am working a lot and I am trying to forget poor Lucy. But this story is not finished. Van Helsing came into my office with an article from *The Westminster Gazette*.

'What do you think about that?' he asked.

I read about the children being taken away by the 'bloofer lady' and about the punctures on their necks. 'Well?' Van Helsing said.

'They are like the punctures on poor Lucy's throat,' I said.

'And what do you think about it?' he asked.

'Well,' I said, 'I think that whatever caused the punctures on Lucy's neck caused the punctures on the children's neck.'

'That is true indirectly, but not directly,' he said.

'Professor, I don't understand,' I said.

Then he said, 'Do you think that the holes in the children's throats were made by the same thing that made the holes in Lucy's throat?'

'Yes, I believe so,' I replied.

'Then you are wrong. It is much, much worse,' he said.

'What are you talking about, Professor?' I shouted.

'The holes in the children's necks were made by Lucy!'

At first I was very angry and I said, 'Dr Van Helsing, are you mad?'

He looked at me calmly and said, 'Tonight, I can prove it to you. Do you have the courage to come with me to the graveyard to check Lucy's tomb?'

At 10 o'clock that evening we went secretly to Lucy's tomb. It was empty!

We waited and waited outside the tomb. Suddenly, we saw something white moving through the trees. The white thing then disappeared. Van Helsing then found a small child. He brought it to me and said, 'Do you believe me now?'

'No,' I said aggressively because I did not want to see the horrible truth.

27 September

Van Helsing and I returned to Lucy's tomb. He opened her coffin again, and Lucy was there! She was more beautiful than ever. Van Helsing showed me her pointed teeth but I still couldn't believe him. He then told me that Lucy was now Un-Dead [2] or Nosferatu as they call the Un-Dead in Eastern Europe. She could not die because the vampire had bitten her. She needed our help to really die and be free. I asked him what we had to do to free Lucy.

'We will cut off her head and fill her mouth with garlic and then we will drive a stake through her body.'

2. **Un-Dead** : the prefix 'un' generally means 'not'; 'Un-Dead' is unusual since we would simple say 'alive' for the opposite of 'dead' so, this word gives us the idea of something that is not dead, but not alive — in other words, a vampire.

'But,' he continued, 'Arthur must do this terrible thing or he will never believe it. He will think we killed her, or that Lucy was buried alive.'

29 September

Arthur, Quincey and I went to see Van Helsing. Van Helsing explained to Arthur about the Un-Dead, and what he must do to Lucy's body. At first, Arthur was very angry, but in the end he agreed to come with us to Lucy's tomb.

That night we went to Lucy's tomb. Before opening the coffin, Van Helsing said, 'John, last night, was Lucy's body in here?' I said yes and then he opened the coffin. It was empty. We then went outside to wait. Dr Van Helsing put pieces of Sacred Wafer around the entrance of the tomb.

'What are you doing?' asked Quincey.

'I am closing the tomb, so that the Un-Dead cannot enter,' he answered.

Then we went behind some trees and waited. After some time we saw a woman arrive. We could not see her face, but she was holding a child. She came closer and in the moonlight we could see her face clearly. It was Lucy! But her sweetness had gone. Now she was hard, cruel and voluptuous. Her lips were red with blood and there was blood on her chin and her white clothes.

When she saw us, she moved back and made a sound like an angry cat. In that moment my love for Lucy became hate. She then threw the child on the ground and began to move towards Arthur.

'Come to me, Arthur,' she said, 'Leave these others and come to me. My arms are hungry for you. Come, and we can rest together. Come, my husband, come!'

The Bloofer Woman

There was something diabolically sweet about her voice. Arthur started walking towards her and she went quickly towards him. But Van Helsing jumped between them and held a gold crucifix at her. She became furious and Van Helsing continued to hold up the crucifix. Then he said to Arthur, 'My friend, can I do what I told you?'

Arthur covered his face with his hands and said, 'Yes, do what you must do.'

Then Van Helsing put the crucifix away and took the Sacred Wafer away from the entrance of the tomb. We all watched in horror as the woman went through a thin crack into the tomb.

The next night we all went back to the tomb. Van Helsing opened the coffin again and there was the beautiful body of Lucy.

'Is this really Lucy's body, or some demon in her shape?' Arthur asked.

'It is her body, and yet it is not her body,' explained Van Helsing. 'Arthur, you must set her free.'

Arthur agreed to do it, and Van Helsing gave him a stake and a hammer.

'Put the stake over her heart,' said Van Helsing, 'and hit it with this hammer. I will say a prayer for the dead. When you have finished, Lucy can finally have true peace.'

Arthur put the point of the stake over the heart, and Quincey, Van Helsing and I began to read the prayer. Then Arthur hit the stake as hard as he could.

The Thing in the coffin moved about and screamed horribly. Its pointed teeth came together on the lips until blood came out. But Arthur did not stop. He hit the stake and hit the stake, and finally the body stopped moving That horrible creature was not there anymore. The real Lucy was there.

The text and **beyond**

1 **Comprehension check**

Match the quotes below with the character who said them, and then match the quotes with the reason why they said them.
Each character may have said more than one quote.

Who

Lucy (L)   Arthur (A)   Jack (J)   Van Helsing (V)

What

1 ☐ ☐ 'My God! My God!'
2 ☐ ☐ 'Hold her hand — it will comfort her more.'
3 ☐ ☐ 'Oh my love, I am so happy you have come!'
4 ☐ ☐ 'Protect Arthur and give me peace.'
5 ☐ ☐ 'No, this is only the beginning.'
6 ☐ ☐ 'Dr Van Helsing, are you mad?'
7 ☐ ☐ 'No.'
8 ☐ ☐ 'He will think we killed her, or that Lucy was buried alive.'
9 ☐ ☐ 'Yes, do what you must do.'
10 ☐ ☐ 'Arthur, you must set her free.'

Why

A She wants to bite Arthur.
B Her non-vampire part wants her vampire part to be killed.
C He is now convinced that his fiancée is a vampire.
D He has just been told that the woman he loved is a vampire.
E He knows that Lucy is now a vampire.
F He refuses to accept the truth about Lucy's condition.
G He is explaining why they have to have Arthur kill the vampire.
H He is telling him to drive a stake into her heart.
I He has just seen the sign that Lucy is about to die.
J He wants to keep a vampire from biting Arthur.

90

2 Fill in the gaps

For questions 1-9, read the text below and think of the word which best fits each space. Use only one word in each space. There is an example at the beginning (0).

Dracula faces the woman question

Dracula is, of course, an entertaining horror story, (**0**) ..something.... to read late at night. (**1**) .... it also speaks about the real worries and anxieties of its author and his time. (**2**) .... of the biggest worries of the day was the 'new woman', or, as we would now say, the liberated woman. Mina, in the original novel, refers to this 'new woman' several times. She says that in the future the 'new woman' will propose marriage to a man — the roles of women and men will be (**3**) .... upside down. Many in Victorian England (1837-1901) thought (**4**) .... a woman's place was in the home. Or as the poet Alfred Lord Tennyson (1809-92) wrote in his poem *The Princess*:

> *Man for the field and woman for the hearth**
> *Man for the sword and for the needle she:*
> *Man with the head and woman with the heart:*
> *Man to command and woman to obey.*

But with the new industrial age, the roles of (**5**) .... men and women had to change: women were needed in the factories. The whole problem of women at work, in the home and in society was then (**6**) .... the 'woman question'. The philosopher John Stuart Mill (1806-73) wrote in his famous essay *The Subjection of Women* that 'the nature of woman is eminently an artificial thing — the result of forced repression in some directions, unnatural stimulation in others.'

In *Dracula* Stoker shows how 'the nature of woman' (**7**) .... be transformed. He also gives a contradictory view of women: Lucy, (**8**) .... in many ways is a 'new woman', changes into a vampire and then wishes to control and dominate men. Mina, too, (**9**) .... things in common with the 'new woman', but her courage and intelligence are always at the service of her man.

1. **hearth** : the fireplace, but here it means the home.

3 Sentence transformation

For questions 1-8, complete the second sentence so that it has a similar meaning to the first sentence, using the word given. Do not change the word given. You must use between two and five words, including the word given. There is an example at the beginning (0).

0 We prepared ourselves for another blood transfusion.
ready
We ....*got ready*................ for another blood transfusion.

1 Perhaps a rat or a small dog made these punctures.
may
A rat or a small dog .... these punctures.

2 Arthur Holmwood gave me permission to read all of Lucy's letters.
let
Arthur Holmwood .... all of Lucy's letters.

3 'What do you think about that?' he asked me.
I
He asked me .... about it.

4 Do you have the courage to come with me to the graveyard to check Lucy's tomb?
courageous
Are you .... to come with me to the graveyard to check Lucy's tomb?

5 Her sweetness had gone.
not
Her sweetness .... there.

6 Mr Hawkins thinks it would be a good idea, if we married there.
marry
Mr Hawkins thinks .... there.

7 I am not able to understand her problem.
wrong
I do not know .... her.

8 If blood had come out of those two punctures, Lucy's bed would have been full of blood.
could
Blood .... out of those two punctures because Lucy's bed was not full of blood.

FCE **4** Speaking

In pairs, look at these photographs of women. Compare them and say which of the photographs corresponds to the usual role of women in your country. What do you think should be the role of women? Has the role of women changed from when your grandmothers were young women? How?

Before you read

1 Vocabulary

Match the pictures (A-C) to the words (1-3). You can use a dictionary to help you.

A
B
C

1 moth   **2** owl   **3** fox

CHAPTER **SIX**

Battle Plans

 www.blackcat-cideb.com

Dr Seward's Diary

30 September

Mr Jonathan Harker arrived at the asylum at nine o'clock. He is very intelligent and full of energy. If his diary is true, then he must also be very courageous.

Later

Mr Harker and Mina went to their room after lunch. I can hear the noise of the typewriter. They are putting together all the evidence we have from our diaries in chronological order. Mr Harker has information about the Count's boxes and where they were sent in England. I wonder what he will think of my diaries.

Battle Plans

It is strange that I never thought of this before, but the Count may be in the house called Carfax which is next to the asylum. This would certainly explain Renfield's strange behaviour.

30 September

Today Mina asked me if she could see Mr Renfield.

She said, 'You have written so many interesting things about him.'

I then went to Renfield and told him that a lady wanted to see him. He was not happy about this but he said, 'Oh, very well, bring her, but wait a moment. I want to tidy up my room.' His way of tidying up was very peculiar. He took all the spiders and flies from his boxes and simply swallowed [1] them. When he had finished he said happily, 'Let the lady come in.'

When Mina Harker came into Renfield's cell she said, 'Good evening, Mr Renfield. Dr Seward has told me many things about you.'

'You're not the girl that the doctor wanted to marry, are you?' Renfield said. 'You can't be, you know, because she's dead.'

Mina smiled and said, 'Oh no! I have a husband.'

'Then what are you doing here?' asked Renfield.

'My husband and I are visiting Dr Seward,' she answered.

'Then don't stay.'

Finally we had to go and Mrs Harker said, 'Good-bye, Mr Renfield, I hope I can see you often and in happier conditions.'

'Good-bye, my dear,' answered Renfield, 'I pray to God that I will never see your sweet face again. May God bless you and protect you!'

---

1   **swallowed them** : put them in his mouth and sent them towards his stomach.

Mina Harker's Diary
30 September

Today Dr Van Helsing has arrived. We all met in Dr Seward's study to decide how we were going to fight the Count. We all sat at a table. There was Arthur, Quincey, Dr John Seward, Jonathan, Dr Van Helsing and myself. Van Helsing said, 'Vampires become stronger and stronger after they suck blood. The vampire we must fight, Count Dracula, is as strong as twenty men. He is very intelligent and he can call the dead for help. He can appear where he wants and he can change shape. He can direct the rain, the fog and thunder. He can command animals like rats, owls, bats, moths, foxes and wolves. He can grow and he can become small. He can see in the dark. It will be a very difficult fight, but we must win.'

We all made a solemn pact to fight and destroy the Count.

'Well,' continued Dr Van Helsing, 'we also have our strengths. We have science. We have friendship and love. We can act during the day and night, and we are free. The vampire is not free. He cannot enter a house when he wants. Somebody must invite him first, and only then can he come and go as he wants. Also, he must sleep in the boxes of earth he brought from his castle. His power ends during the day. In addition certain things hurt him, such as garlic, a crucifix. You can kill him, as we have seen, by driving a stake through his heart and cutting off his head.

We must find all the boxes of earth, and when we are ready, we must kill or capture the monster. If we don't find him in one of the boxes, we must sterilise them by putting a piece of Sacred Wafer in them so he cannot go back in them. Then in the end, we must find him between sunrise and sunset when he is weakest.

Now, finally, Madam Mina, your part in this terrible story is finished. We will tell you nothing about our plans until we have killed Dracula. We cannot risk your life. We will be freer to act if we know that you are not in danger.'

All the men seemed happy about this. Now they have gone to Carfax to look for the Count's boxes of earth.

Dr Seward's Diary
1 October, 4 a.m.

We were leaving the house to go to Carfax, when one of my assistants brought me a message from Renfield. He said that he had to speak with me immediately.

Arthur, Quincey, Dr Van Helsing and I went to his cell. He spoke to us very calmly and intelligently. Then he asked me if he could leave the asylum. I told him that he seemed much better and that I would consider his request very carefully.

'You do not understand,' he said, 'I must leave the asylum tonight. It is very important.'

'Why do you want to leave?' asked Dr Van Helsing.

'I am sorry, but I cannot tell you,' replied Renfield.

I then walked to the door of his cell and said, 'Come, my friends, we have work to do. Good night, Mr Renfield.'

The text and **beyond**

FCE **1** **Comprehension check**

For questions 1-5, choose the best answer — A, B, C or D.

1 Arthur, Quincey, Mina, Jonathan and Van Helsing came to the lunatic asylum to

- A ☐ look for the Count.
- B ☐ make plans to kill the Count.
- C ☐ meet Seward's patient, Renfield.
- D ☐ read and discuss Jack's diaries.

2 Renfield ate his spiders because

- A ☐ he wanted to become stronger.
- B ☐ he was going to receive a guest.
- C ☐ he wanted Dr Seward to let him leave.
- D ☐ he didn't like them anymore.

3 Renfield did not want to see Mina again because

- A ☐ he liked her and wanted her to be safe.
- B ☐ he didn't like women visitors.
- C ☐ she was not Dr Seward's fiancée.
- D ☐ he did not want to keep his room tidy.

4 Van Helsing said the Sacred Wafers could be used to

- A ☐ find the Count's boxes of earth.
- B ☐ kill the Count when he was in a box of earth.
- C ☐ keep the Count from changing shape.
- D ☐ keep the Count from using his boxes of earth.

5 Which of the following was NOT going to help the Count?

- A ☐ Jonathan, Jack, and Quincey
- B ☐ different animals like moths and rats
- C ☐ his ability to change size
- D ☐ the dead

2 Word square
Fill in the gaps below and then find those words in the word square.

Medicine

_ e i _ _

_ _ _ _ _ f u _ _ _ _

_ a r c _ _ _ _

_ e v e r

I _ _

Animals and how they move and sound

_ _ i d _ r

_ _ a p p _ _ g

_ a _

_ o w _

_ o t _

_ _ x

Vampire things

_ o f _ _ _

_ _ r l _ _

p _ _ _ _ u r _ _

_ t _ k _

Head and face

f _ _ _ h _ _ _

_ i p _

_ h r _ a _

c h _ _

```
T  T  H  I  S  W  I  L  L  R  E  F  A  L  L
M  R  A  V  E  I  N  S  K  E  Y  L  O  N  O
S  L  A  B  C  B  O  A  T  W  A  A  P  A  P
L  P  A  N  U  O  F  E  V  E  R  P  U  R  L
P  I  I  G  S  H  F  O  S  T  W  P  N  C  J
I  A  P  D  E  F  A  F  U  S  T  I  C  O  T
L  J  A  S  E  B  U  I  I  Z  O  N  T  T  H
L  O  G  A  R  R  D  S  E  N  V  G  U  I  R
A  M  P  I  R  E  S  A  I  Y  O  U  R  C  O
C  H  I  N  S  U  R  E  T  O  T  H  E  S  A
F  A  T  B  A  T  R  A  I  N  N  G  S  R  T
E  A  S  Y  R  A  B  E  A  T  L  J  R  A  S
P  H  O  W  L  D  A  N  M  O  T  H  U  G  L
C  L  O  S  E  D  M  I  S  U  N  D  E  R  S
S  F  O  X  S  F  O  R  E  H  E  A  D  S  M
```

3 Hot seat

Students will take it in turns to be Count Dracula, Jonathan Harker, Mina Murray, Renfield or Professor Van Helsing. These students will sit in the 'hot seat'. The rest of the class will interview him or her. The answers should reflect the facts of the story, but you will also have to use your imagination. Below are some questions you can use, but you can also invent some more.

Questions for Count Dracula

- Why did you decide to invade England first and not, for example, France or Italy?
- What do you think of Mr Harker?
- What do you think about Van Helsing? Do you think he is a worthy adversary?

Questions for Jonathan Harker

- Do you ever think that this situation with Dracula is unreal, just a dream?
- Do you think that other people, outside your group of friends, will ever believe your story?
- What frightens you the most about the Count?

Questions for Mina Murray

- Did you ever think that Jonathan was crazy, or that he had invented the story about vampires for some reason?
- Are you afraid for your own life?
- Why do you think the Count decided to attack your friend Lucy?

Questions for Renfield

- Have you always been obsessed with lives — flies, spiders, kittens and other animals?
- Why do you consider Dracula your 'master'?
- Why are you afraid for Mina Murray?

Questions for Professor Van Helsing

- Is this the first time that you have ever fought a vampire?
- Do you think that Count Dracula is the only vampire in England or Europe?
- Why did you first become interested in vampires?

 **Fill in the gaps**

For questions 1-9 read the text below and decide which answer (A, B, C or D) best fits each space. There is an example at the beginning (0).

The summer when modern horror was born

June of 1816 was cold and (0) ..D.. . In fact, 1816 is known in history as 'the year without summer'. Scientists believe that volcanic explosions had sent dust into that atmosphere which blocked the sun (1) .... to lower the temperatures. For poor farmers around the world it was a year of desperation. But for a group of young people (2) .... in the Villa Diodati along the shores of Lake Geneva in Switzerland it meant boredom (this is where the poet John Milton — the creator of the great poetic character of Satan in the epic poem *Paradise Lost* — stayed in 1639). These young people included the poets Lord Byron (1788-1824) and Percy Bysshe Shelley (1792-1822), the novelist Mary Shelley (1797-1851), along with Byron's personal doctor John Polidori and Mary Shelley's half-sister Claire Clairmont. To fight the boredom, they began to read German ghost stories (3) .... loud, and then one day Byron said, 'We will each write a ghost story.' Byron wrote part of a story which he called 'The Fragment'. Polidori wrote a story that was terrible and Shelley produced a bit of poetry. Clearly the best was Mary Shelley's story about a scientist who (4) .... to bring back to life pieces of dead bodies to make a monster. She later worked on her little story and it (5) .... the novel *Frankenstein*, which was first published in 1818. Its influence on modern culture has (6) .... enormous. But this is not the end of our tale because Polidori later added to Byron's fragment and produced a short story called *The Vampyre*. Polidori's story is certainly not a great work of art like *Frankenstein*, (7) .... it created the modern myth of the vampire — the one we all know from hundreds of films and books. Before Polidori's story, the vampire was a creature of folklore. But Polidori's vampire was an elegant and evil aristocrat named Lord Ruthven. This was also the name of the protagonist of a novel by Lady Caroline Lamb; and her protagonist was clearly inspired by Lord Byron. Byron was the most notorious celebrity of his time. Indeed Byron, as Caroline Lamb famously wrote, was 'Mad — bad — dangerous to know.' *The Vampyre* was a (8) .... success. It inspired operas and novels. So, Lord Ruthven — a (9) .... of supernatural Lord Byron — was the literary ancestor of the Transylvanian Count Dracula, and the first of the intelligent, cruel and refined vampires which have dominated the modern world's imagination.

0	A rained	B raining	C rain	D rainy
1	A much	B so	C enough	D very
2	A staying	B resting	C being	D remaining
3	A out	B to	C in	D by
4	A succeed	B manages	C can	D able
5	A grew	B was	C became	D turns
6	A been	B got	C developed	D happened
7	A although	B however	C anyway	D but
8	A very	B much	C large	D great
9	A kind	B style	C class	D variety

Before you read

1 Reading pictures
Look at the picture on page 107 and discuss these questions.

1   Describe the picture. Where is the Count?
2   What is he holding?
3   The Count is offering this to somebody. Who do you think he is offering it to and why?

Look at the picture on page 111 and discuss these questions.

1   Describe the scene. What do you think is happening? Why?
2   Talk about the characters. How do you think they are feeling?
3   What do you think will happen next?

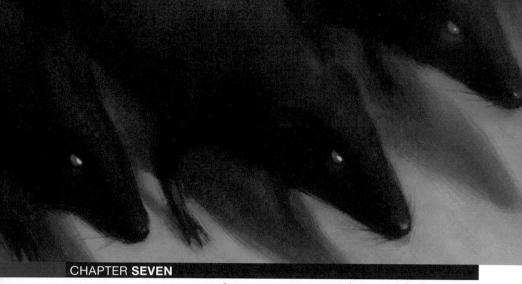

'The Girls You Love Are Mine'

 www.blackcat-cideb.com

Jonathan Harker's Diary

1 October, 5 a.m.

I was very relaxed when we went to Carfax because Mina's part in this horrible business is finished. But still Renfield had upset us with his strange request.

Quincey came and showed us a silver whistle. 'Carfax may be full of rats so I brought this whistle. If any rats come, I will blow this whistle and my dogs will come.'

Then Dr Van Helsing gave us each a silver crucifix and a piece of the Sacred Wafer. Dr Seward opened the door of Carfax and then we went to the chapel. Everything was covered with dust and the air had a terrible odour: the odour of blood and decay. [1]

'The first thing we must do,' said Dr Van Helsing, 'is to see how many boxes of earth are left.'

---

1. **decay** : decomposition.

'The Girls You Love Are Mine'

We found only twenty-nine of the original fifty boxes!

Then we noticed lots of shining little points, like lots of little stars. They were the eyes of rats, thousands and thousands of rats! Arthur blew the whistle and his dogs ran into the chapel. At first they seemed frightened, but after a moment they attacked the rats and killed many of them. The other rats ran away.

When I returned to our room, I found Mina sleeping. She looked paler than usual.

2 October, evening

We have begun looking for the missing boxes. We found a man who said that he took nine great boxes to a house in Piccadilly. We must go there and sterilise the boxes.

Dr Seward's Diary
3 October

I must write exactly what happened last night. We were all discussing the Count's other hiding places when we heard a scream. An attendant ran into the room and said that he had found Renfield on the floor all covered with blood. We ran to Renfield's room and found him on the floor. We could see that Renfield was dying because he was breathing with great difficulty.

Suddenly Renfield opened his eyes and said, 'I have had a terrible dream, and it has left me so weak that I can't move. What is wrong with my face? What is all this blood?'

'Tell us about your dream,' said Dr Van Helsing very calmly.

Renfield continued, 'I must not deceive myself. It was not a dream. It was real. The Count came up to the window in the mist as he had done many times before. But this time he was solid. He was laughing with his red mouth, and his sharp white teeth were shining in the moonlight. At first I did not invite him to come in — you know that if I do not invite him, he can't come in so he started to promise me things. He began to whisper, "Rats, rats, rats! Hundreds, thousands, millions of them and every one a life; and dogs to eat them and cats too. All lives!" I laughed at him because I wanted to see what he could do. He told me to come to the window. I could see that there were thousands of rats with red eyes like his, only smaller. "I will give you all these lives if you worship me," [2] he said. And then a red mist like blood covered my eyes, and, before I knew what I was doing, I was opening the window and saying to Him, "Come in, Lord and Master!"'

Mr Renfield's voice grew weaker so we gave him some brandy.

'The next day,' he continued, 'I waited for the rats, but the Count didn't send me anything, not even a fly. Then that evening he came again without asking me. I got angry with him but I could not stop him. I thought, for some strange reason, that Mrs Harker had come into my room.'

At this point, we all came closer to Mr Renfield, but he didn't pay attention and continued speaking.

'When Mrs Harker came into my room this afternoon,' Renfield continued, 'she was not the same, she was paler. I don't like pale people very much. I like them with lots of blood in them, and she seemed to have lost all of hers. It made me angry to think that the Count was taking all of the blood out of Mrs

2. **worship me** : adore me like a god.

Harker. So when he came tonight, I was ready for him. I fought him, but he was too strong for me. He threw me down on the floor. Then I saw the red cloud and heard a loud noise, and he left the room.'

We all ran to Mrs Harker's room. The door was locked so we had to break in. Then we saw something truly horrible.

The moonlight was bright enough, so we could see Jonathan Harker lying unconscious on the bed. Mina was kneeling on the bed facing the other direction. In front of her was the Count who was pushing her face into his chest. There was a cut on his chest and blood came out. He was forcing her to drink the blood. He looked at us and his eyes burned with evil passion. The Professor, holding the Sacred Wafer, walked towards him, and we were behind him holding the silver crucifixes. Just then a cloud covered the moon, and when the light came back the Count had disappeared.

We then went to help Mina who suddenly screamed in such a terrible way that I will never forget it. Her face was pale and her lips and cheeks and chin were covered with red blood. She then began to cry.

Dr Van Helsing woke Jonathan up with some cold water. When he woke up he saw Mina covered with blood and he shouted, 'In God's name, what does this mean? What has happened? Mina, dear, what is it? Good God, help us, help her!'

Then Dr Van Helsing turned to Mina and said, 'Mina, poor dear Mina, you must tell us exactly what happened.'

Mina trembled and began, 'I took the sleeping medicine Dr Van Helsing had given me, but I still couldn't sleep. I kept thinking about death, blood and vampires. Finally, I fell asleep and did not even wake up when Jonathan came into the room to sleep. Then I remember seeing a white mist in the room and I felt terror. Then it seemed as if the mist had become a tall, thin man dressed in black. I recognised the Count and I wanted to scream, but he said, "Silence, if you make a sound I will take him and crush his brain out in front of you."

Then with a smile on his face, he pushed my head back to expose my throat. "Be quiet," he said, "because this is not the first time that I drink your blood."'

Jonathan groaned [3] and held onto Mina's hand, and Mina continued, 'Then he said, "So you thought you could stop me? Your friends should have watched you more carefully instead of looking for me. And now you are mine. When my brain says 'Come!' to you, you will cross land or sea to do what I command." Then he opened his shirt and with his long nails he made a cut. When the blood came out he pushed my mouth against the blood. I had to swallow it. Oh my God! What have I done? What have I done?'

Jonathan Harker's Diary
3 October
We all met again to discuss our plans for destroying the Count's boxes of earth. We decided that we should first sterilise the boxes at Carfax before going to his hiding place in Piccadilly.

Before we left to go to Carfax Professor Van Helsing said, 'Now my dear friends we are going out on a terrible mission. Are

---

3. **groaned**: made a sound like 'ooooh!' because he was suffering.

we all armed to fight that monster?' We said yes. 'Then all is well,' he continued, 'and you Mina will be safe here until we return. I have put things in your room so that he can't enter. Now let me protect you. I will touch your forehead with this piece of the Sacred Wafer in the name of the Father, the Son, and...'

When he touched Mina's forehead with the Sacred Wafer, Mina screamed in a horrible way because the Wafer had burned her forehead as if it were white-hot metal. Mina understood immediately the meaning and shouted, 'Unclean! [4] I am unclean now! Even God refuses me!'

'One day,' said Dr Van Helsing calmly, 'God will remove that red scar [5] from your forehead. Perhaps we are instruments of God and we must suffer as Christ suffered.'

It was then time for us to go to Carfax and sterilise the boxes.

We put a Sacred Wafer in each of the boxes in the chapel at Carfax, and then we went to the house in Piccadilly. There we found only eight of the nine boxes that we were looking for. Fortunately we found some papers and some keys with labels. On these labels were the addresses of the Count's other houses. Arthur and Quincey went to these other houses, and we had to wait.

Dr Seward's Diary

3 October

The time seemed to pass terribly slowly.

Just then somebody knocked at the door. It was a telegraph

4. **unclean** : not clean (here, in a spiritual sense).
5. **scar** : mark remaining where the skin was hurt.

boy and he gave us a telegram from Mina that said, 'Be careful! It is 12.45 now and Dracula is going South to the house in Piccadilly where you are.'

'Thank God,' said Van Helsing, 'we will soon meet him. Let us hope that Arthur and Quincey arrive here before him.'

Then after a few minutes we heard another knock at the door. Luckily it was Quincey and Arthur.

'It's all right,' said Arthur, 'we found both hiding places with twelve boxes and we destroyed them all.'

We then told them that the Count was coming and we prepared ourselves for his arrival. After a few minutes we heard slow steps outside the room, and then the Count leaped into the room like a panther.

Jonathan placed himself in front of the door so that the Count could not escape.

Only Jonathan lifted up his giant Kukri knife and tried to stab [6] the Count, but the Count was too quick. But Jonathan did cut the Count's coat and a lot of banknotes and gold coins fell on the floor. I walked toward the Count holding the Crucifix and Wafer in my hand. Jonathan lifted up his arm again to try to stab the Count, but the Count grabbed some of the money and coins from the floor and leaped through the window, breaking the glass.

We ran to the window and looked down at the Count. He turned and spoke to us:

'You think that you have destroyed all my boxes of earth, my resting places. My revenge has just begun. I can live for centuries. Time is on my side. The girls you love are mine

---

6. **stab** : hit with a knife.

already, and with their help you too will be my creatures who will do what I want when I want to feed. Bah!'

And then he disappeared.

'We have learned much,' said Dr Van Helsing after a minute. 'Despite his words, we know that he is afraid of us and that he wants to leave England now.'

We then went back to the house, where Mina was waiting for us. We told her everything that had happened, and then we had dinner. We all did our best to be cheerful, but it was difficult. It was terrible to see that red scar on Mina's forehead. We all knew that even though Mina was for us a symbol of goodness, purity and faith, she was now an outcast[7] from God.

'Jonathan,' she said sweetly, 'I want you and my other friends to remember something in this horrible moment. I know that you must fight and destroy the Count just as you fought and destroyed the false Lucy. But you cannot do this with hate. That poor soul, the Count, who has caused all this misery, is the saddest case of all. Think how happy he will be when his evil part is destroyed and his good part can go to God. You must have pity for him, even when you try to destroy him.'

Jonathan Harker's Diary

4 October

Early this morning before it started getting light, Mina woke me and said, 'Go, call the Professor. I want to see him immediately.'

'Why?' I asked

---

7. **outcast** : someone who has been chased away or sent away because of his bad actions.

'I have an idea,' she said. 'He must hypnotise me before the dawn, and then I will be able to speak.'

When the Professor entered our room, Mina told him to hypnotise her. He told her to sit up in bed and he began. After a few minutes her eyes closed, and then they opened. Then Mina spoke in a strange, sad way that was new to me.

'Where are you,' the Professor asked.

'I don't know. It is all strange to me,' she replied.

'What do you see?' he asked

'I can see nothing. It is all dark,' she replied.

'What do you hear?' asked the Professor.

'I can hear the sound of water on the outside,' she said.

'Then you are on a ship?' Van Helsing continued.

'Oh, yes!' Mina replied 'I can hear men walking above me.'

'What are you doing?' asked Van Helsing.

'I am still — oh, so still. It is like death!' And then Mina stopped talking. The sun had already risen. We asked the Professor what this all meant.

'When the Count forced Mina to drink his blood — her baptism of blood! — he won control over her mind. When he wants, he can call her telepathically, but at dawn and at sunset I can hypnotise Mina and read the Count's mind. Now we know that he is escaping! He saw that he cannot stay in London with only one box of earth. He must return to his castle in Transylvania.'

The text and **beyond**

1 Comprehension check

Match the phrases in column A with those in column B to make true sentences. There are two phrases in column B that you do not need to use.

A

1. ☐ Jonathan and his friends knew there were rats around them
2. ☐ Renfield laughed at the Count
3. ☐ Jonathan and his friends gave Renfield something to drink
4. ☐ The second day the Count entered without an invitation
5. ☐ Renfield realized that the Count was drinking Mina's blood
6. ☐ Renfield attacked the Count
7. ☐ Mina did not scream when she saw the Count
8. ☐ The Wafer burned Mina
9. ☐ Van Helsing hypnotised Mina
10. ☐ Van Helsing and his friends were certain the Count was leaving England
11. ☐ The Count had to go back to his castle
12. ☐ The Count said he would give Renfield many rats

B

A because they wanted to hear the end of his story.
B because he wanted to be invited into the asylum.
C because she was becoming a vampire herself.
D because almost all his earth in London was sterilised.
E because they could see the reflection of their eyes in the light.
F because Mina could hear the sound of water.
G because he wanted to see if the Count really could give him animals.
H because she had lost all the colour in her face.
I because she did not want him to kill Jonathan.
J because Renfield had already asked him in the day before.
K because they could hear them and smell them.
L because she was already a vampire.
M because her thoughts were connected with those of the Count.
N because he wanted to save Mina.

115

FCE ② Carmilla: the vampire that enchanted Bram Stoker

Another important literary influence on Bram Stoker was the huge book (about 1800 pages!) *Varney the Vampire, or The Feast of Blood* by James Rymper.

However, emotionally, Stoker was very much influenced by the short story of a fellow Irishman named Sheridan Le Fanu (1814-73). His story is called *Carmilla*. It tells of a woman vampire: the strangely romantic side of this story is very disturbing.

You are going to read a short version of *Carmilla*. Seven sentences have been removed from the article. Choose from the sentences A-G the one which fits each gap (1-6). There is one extra sentence which you do not need to use.

A rich Englishman lived with his daughter Laura in a castle in Styria — a province of Austria that borders on Hungary. (**1**) .... When Laura was six years old she dreamed of a beautiful and mysterious visitor who came to her in the middle of the night. She also said that she was bitten on the chest.

One evening when Laura was 18, she and her father were outside the castle admiring the sunset. Her father had just received a letter from his friend General Spielsdorf. (**2**) .... However, he would explain everything later. They saw a carriage drive by and then the carriage had an accident. A woman from the carriage ran up to Laura and her father. She said that she had urgent business and must leave. She asked if she could leave her daughter, Carmilla, who was Laura's age. (**3**) .... Laura and her father were happy to have the guest. Laura and Carmilla became very close friends. At times, however, Carmilla seemed too affectionate. She would say to Laura, 'You are mine, you will be, and you and I are one forever.' Carmilla always slept during the day, and she seemed to sleepwalk at night. Then one day some pictures of the ancestors of Laura's mother arrived. Her father had sent them away to be cleaned. (**4**) ....

Then Laura began to get ill. She also saw at night a strange creature like a cat that bit her on the chest. (**5**) .... At this time Laura and her father took a carriage to the abandoned village of Karnstein. On their way there, they met General Spielsdorf. He told them how his niece had met a young woman at a costume ball. Her name was Millarca. She, just like Carmilla, had a strange mother who had to leave on urgent business. She left Millarca with the General and his niece. Later the General learned that Millarca was really a vampire. But his niece died and the vampire escaped.

Now, the General was going to Karnstein to look for the tomb of the vampire. So, the General, Laura and her father all went to the tomb of the vampire. When they arrived, they met a very strange man. This man was Baron Vordenburg, an expert in vampires. They then opened the tomb of the Countess Mircalla. (6) ....This was the end of Mircalla-Carmilla-Millarca the vampire. Still, for the rest of her life, Laura had the feeling that Carmilla was going to return. At times she could almost hear Carmilla's footsteps.

A A doctor told her father that Laura should never sleep alone.
B Strangely, Carmilla looked exactly like the picture of the Countess Mircalla Karnstein, who had been dead for 200 years.
C She promised to return in three months.
D They drove a stake through the vampire's heart and then cut off its head.
E She told them that her daughter was really a vampire.
F His wife, who was dead, had been from a noble Hungarian family.
G The general wrote that his niece, who had planned to come and stay with Laura, was dead.

Carmilla (1993) by Jonathan Barry.

Before you read

1 Listening

Listen to the first part of Chapter Eight. You will hear about the beginning of the pursuit of Count Dracula. For questions 1-5, choose the best answer — A, B or C.

1 It was easy to find the Count's ship because
   A ☐ just one ship carried boxes to the Black Sea.
   B ☐ just one ship was travelling to the Black Sea.
   C ☐ only a few ships carried boxes to the Black Sea.

2 In the end, the *Czarina Catherine* ended its journey
   A ☐ at Varna.
   B ☐ at Galatz.
   C ☐ in the Dardanelles.

3 Mina and Van Helsing went to the port to talk with
   A ☐ some Slovaks.
   B ☐ the captain of the ship.
   C ☐ a man named Skinsky.

4 Mina knew that the Count was travelling on a river because
   A ☐ Skinsky told them that Slovaks travelled by river.
   B ☐ Mina heard flowing water when she was hypnotised.
   C ☐ Mina heard the Count mention a river when she was hypnotised.

5 Mina was going to travel to the Count's castle with
   A ☐ Quincey.
   B ☐ Jonathan.
   C ☐ Van Helsing.

Racing against the Sun

Mina Harker's Diary

5 October, 5 p.m.

The men have discovered the ship that is taking the Count back to Transylvania. It was not difficult to find because there was only one ship that was going towards the Black Sea. It is called the *Czarina Catherine*. The box containing the Count is being taken to the port of Varna on the Black Sea.

Dr Seward's Diary

28 October

We left Charing Cross on the morning of the twelfth and got to Paris the same night. Then we took the Orient Express east. We travelled night and day, and arrived here in Varna on the fifteenth.

119

Then on 25 October we received news that the *Czarina Catherine* was going through the Dardanelles.

Finally, today we received a telegram saying the *Czarina Catherine* had entered the port of Galatz, which is further north on the Black Sea. The Count has tricked us!

Mina Harker's Diary

30 October

When we arrived here in Galatz we went directly to the port to see the captain of the *Czarina Catherine*. He told us that fog had surrounded the *Czarina Catherine* for most of its voyage, and that it had travelled incredibly fast. In addition, mysteriously, it had arrived at Galatz instead of Varna. We then discovered that the box of earth containing the Count was no longer on the boat. A man named Skinsky had taken it. Skinksy, who was later found killed, then gave the box to some Slovaks.

When I am hypnotised I can hear the sound of moving water. Therefore, we know that the Count is on a river. The river that flows closest to his castle is the Sereth. We must try to catch him on the river. It will be easier to destroy him there because vampires cannot cross running water on their own.

We have decided to follow the Count separately. I will go with Professor Van Helsing by train to the town of Veresti. At Veresti we will take a carriage and go to the Count's castle. Arthur and Jonathan will go in a steam launch [1] up the Sereth river and try to catch up to [2] the Count's boat. Quincey and John will follow them

---

1. **steam launch** : a large motor boat; in this case the motor is powered by steam (vapour).
2. **catch up to** : reach someone or something that is going ahead of you.

on horses on the banks of the river. All of us have guns and knives because we know that there will be a fight. The Slovaks will try to stop us.

2 November, night

We have been travelling all day. The country is getting wilder, and we are getting closer to the Carpathians. Dr Van Helsing says that we will reach the Borgo Pass by morning.

We are going to the place where my dear Jonathan suffered so much!

Abraham Van Helsing's Diary
5 November, morning

I must write down accurately everything. We travelled all day yesterday. At around sunset I saw the Count's castle as Jonathan had described it in his diary. I was both happy and afraid, because I knew that the end was near.

We stopped the carriage and I prepared a fire and something to eat. I gave some to Mina, but she did not eat. I was afraid that Mina was changing so I drew a circle with the Sacred Wafer around where Mina was sitting. While I was doing this Mina did not move or say a word, but she became whiter and whiter. When I walked into the circle, Mina held onto me, and I could feel that she was shaking. Then I went out of the circle and went next to the fire.

'Why don't you come over here next to the fire?' I asked her. She stood up and tried to leave the circle, but she stopped.

'Why don't you step out of the circle?' I asked.

'I cannot!' she said.

It was snowing and very cold. I began to get afraid, but I could feel that I was safe inside the circle. I began to see strange shapes forming in the snow. I thought I saw those strange women that had tried to kiss Jonathan. I was afraid for Mina because those strange figures were getting closer, but she was calm and smiled. When I tried to leave the circle, to add more wood to the fire she said, 'No! No! Do not leave the circle. You are safe here.'

'But what about you?' I said.

She laughed a strange laugh and said in a soft voice, 'No one is safer than me!'

I wondered what she meant, but then I saw her red scar in the light of the fire, and I understood. She was safe because she was almost a vampire herself!

Then the three women appeared. They came closer and closer to our circle.

'Come, sister, come to us. Come! Come!' they said to her. I looked at her and saw that there was terror in her eyes. Thank God, she was not like them yet!

And so we waited all night long, with those horrible women around us, and then, at dawn, they disappeared.

5 November, afternoon

I left Mina sleeping in the circle, and I went to the Count's castle. I knew from Jonathan's diary where the chapel was. I had to find at least three graves. I looked and looked, and I finally found one of them. It was the tomb of one of the women I had seen last night. She was so full of life and voluptuous beauty. I

am sure that in the past when a man came to kill a woman vampire, he looked at her beauty, her voluptuous lips, and then he lost courage. He waited and waited, and then sunset arrived and the beautiful eyes of the women opened and the voluptuous mouth opened for a kiss — and man is weak. And then there was one more vampire in the terrible army of the Un-Dead!

It was terrible to think that I had to drive a stake through her heart and cut off her head. I looked at her and something stopped me. I could not move. Then I heard Mina calling me, and I woke up from my trance.

I then went to look for the other two graves. I found another grave, but this time I did not look at her. Then I found a high tomb. In this tomb was the most beautiful of the three. She was so beautiful that I could feel the instinct of man in me. But I was strong. I had now found all three of their tombs, but there was still one more tomb, and it was bigger than all the others. On it there was only one word:

DRACULA

This was the Un-Dead home of the King Vampire. I placed some of the Sacred Wafer in the tomb so that he could never return. Then I began my bloody work with the three women. If I did not remember the look of peace on Lucy's face, I could not have done that horrible thing. They screamed horribly when I drove the stake through their hearts and blood came out of their mouths. Now, those poor souls can have rest!

I then left the Castle and returned to Mina in the circle.

'Come!' she said, 'come away from this terrible place! Let us go to meet my husband who is, I know, coming towards us.'

And so, now we are going towards the east to meet our friends and him whom Mina says that she knows is coming to meet us.

Mina Harker's Diary
6 November

It was late in the afternoon when the Professor and I started to walk toward the east. I knew Jonathan was coming from that direction. We did not move quickly because we had heavy blankets with us: we could not risk being without them in the cold and the snow. We had also brought some food with us. When we had walked about a mile, I sat down to rest. We looked back and saw Dracula's castle against the sky. It was magnificent on the top of the high precipice. There was something wild and strange about this place. We could hear the wolves howling in the distance. They were far away and it was snowing, but the sound was still terrifying. Dr Van Helsing was looking for a protected spot where we could be safe in case the wolves attacked us. After a few minutes, the Professor found a cave in a giant rock. 'See!' he said, 'here you will be protected.' Then he went out with his binoculars and stood on top of the rock. He started looking. Suddenly he called out, 'Look! Look, Mina, look!' I climbed up on top of the rock with him. He gave me the binoculars and pointed. The snow was falling and the wind was blowing. Finally I saw a wagon, and on the wagon was a great square box. My heart jumped because I knew the end was coming. It was late afternoon and sunset was near, when that Thing would be free. A moment later I saw that the Professor had jumped down from the rock and was drawing a circle around it with the Sacred Wafer.

After another moment or so, we could see again and Van Helsing shouted, 'Look! Look! Two men on horses are following the wagon. They are getting closer to it.'

I could see that those two men were John and Quincey, and then I saw two more men racing towards the wagon. One of them was Jonathan and the other was Arthur.

We waited for the wagon to arrive. Every moment seemed like an eternity because we knew that the sun would go down in a few minutes. The wagon was getting closer and closer.

Suddenly we heard two men shout, 'Halt!' One of the men was my Jonathan, the other was Quincey. Even though the men escorting the wagon could not understand the word, they understood the tone of their voice, and stopped their horses. In that moment, Arthur and Jonathan went on one side of the wagon, and John and Quincey went on the other side. The leader of the men gave an order to move. The men on the wagon whipped the horses, but John, Arthur, Quincey and Jonathan raised their Winchester rifles. [3] Then Dr Van Helsing and I appeared from behind the rocks. The men protecting the wagons saw that they were surrounded, so they stopped the horses again.

Then the leader gave another command and his men pulled out knives and pistols. They were ready for our attack. Jonathan and Quincey jumped down from their horses and ran to the wagon. They pushed the men away from the wagon, and in an

3. **Winchester rifle :**
   (This rifle was first produced by Oliver Winchester in 1866).

instant Jonathan jumped onto the wagon, and with incredible strength raised the box and threw it on the ground. Both Quincey and Jonathan then jumped down again and raced to the box. Then I saw that Quincey was holding his side and that blood was coming out, but he did not stop. He continued helping Jonathan pull the lid off the box.

Now, the sun was almost down on the mountain tops. When they had pulled the lid off the box, I could see the Count lying upon the earth. He was terribly pale and his eyes burned with that horrible anger that I knew very well.

As I looked at him, the Count saw the setting sun, and his look of anger became a look of triumph.

But in that moment I saw the flash of Jonathan's great knife. I screamed as I saw it cut through the Count's throat, and in the same moment Quincey's knife went into his heart.

It was like a miracle, but in that very moment the Count's body turned into dust and disappeared.

I will be glad for the rest of my life because in that moment, just before he became dust, I saw a look of peace on the Count's face.

The men rode away quickly in fear.

Quincey had fallen to the ground and was holding his hand against his side, and the blood was flowing out. I jumped down from the rock and ran to him — the circle no longer stopped me.

He was very weak, but he held my hand. Then I am certain that he saw the sadness in my face, because he smiled at me and said, 'I am very happy that I could help you.'

Then suddenly he shouted, 'Oh God!' and sat up and pointed at me. 'Look! Look! It was worth this to die! Look! Look!'

The sun was now directly on top of the mountain, and its light fell on my face. Together, all the men fell on their knees and said, 'Amen' when they looked at me. Then the dying man said, 'Now thank God that all has not been in vain! The red scar has disappeared.'

And then, with a smile and in silence, he died, a brave gentleman.

Note

Seven years ago, we all suffered greatly, but we think that the happiness we have now is worth it. Mina and I have named our little boy Quincey.

This past summer we made a journey to Transylvania. It was almost impossible to believe that what we saw had really existed. Every evidence of those horrors has disappeared.

When we returned, we took out all the papers concerning Count Dracula. We saw that there were hardly any official documents among them. Most of the papers were our own personal diaries. Nobody would accept our personal writings as proof of such an incredible story. Van Helsing, who was then holding our little boy, said this:

'We do not need proof. We do not need anyone to believe us!

This boy will some day know what a brave woman his mother is. Now he knows her sweetness and her love. When he is older he will understand how some men loved her so much that they risked their own lives for her.'

Jonathan Harker

The text and **beyond**

1 Comprehension check

Say whether the following statements are true (T) or false (F), and
then correct the false ones.

		T	F
1	Mina and the men prepared themselves for a fight with the Count's Slovaks.	☐	☐
2	Mina did not leave the circle because she was afraid.	☐	☐
3	Mina was afraid the vampire women would attack her.	☐	☐
4	The vampire women considered Mina their worst enemy.	☐	☐
5	Van Helsing found the courage to kill the vampire women because he hated them.	☐	☐
6	When the Count saw the sun go down, he thought he could still win.	☐	☐
7	The Count died contented.	☐	☐
8	Mina was no longer an outcast of God when the Count died.	☐	☐
9	Jonathan thought their writings would convince people that the Count existed.	☐	☐
10	Transylvania still seemed frightening when Jonathan returned there with his son.	☐	☐

2 Summary

Number the following paragraphs (A-I) in the right order to make a
summary of Chapters 5-8, and then fill in the gaps with the words in
the box.

> wagon   throat   drive   scar   patient   forehead   mind   ground
> asylum   real   scream   pointed   peace   newspapers
> graveyard   carriage   kiss   tricked   tomb   punctures   sunset

A ☐ It was the strange (1) ...., Renfield. They ran to him
and found him covered with blood. He had fought the Count to
protect Mina. The men then went to Mina. They found her in her
room with the Count. She was drinking his blood. The Count
escaped. Then Van Helsing tried to protect Mina by touching
her (2) .... with a Sacred Wafer, but it burned her.

B ☐ Arthur, Jonathan, Mina, Quincey, Van Helsing and Dr Seward all met in the lunatic (**3**) .... to plan their fight against Count Dracula. They decided to find and sterilise all of the Count's boxes of earth. First, they went to Carfax. It was full of rats, but Arthur's dogs killed many of them. They then found twenty-nine of the original fifty boxes. Two days later, while they were discussing the Count's other hiding places, they heard a (**4**) ....

C ☐ After this the men continued destroying his boxes of earth. They almost killed him at his hiding place in Piccadilly. It was obvious that the Count was planning to leave England. Fortunately, Mina realized that if Van Helsing hypnotised her, he could read the Count's (**5**) .... By doing this they realized that the Count was on a ship going towards the Black Sea. They thought he was going to the port of Varna, but he (**6**) .... them and went to the port of Galatz.

D ☐ But this, as Van Helsing said, was only the beginning. Soon the (**7**) .... were speaking about a 'bloofer lady' who took small children away. Van Helsing told Dr Seward that Lucy was actually the 'bloofer lady'. To prove this, he took Dr Seward to the (**8**) .... They went to Lucy's tomb and discovered it was empty. Then they saw something white moving through the trees. Then Van Helsing found a child.

E ☐ Then, just before (**9**) ...., Jonathan cut the Count's (**10**) .... and Quincey drove his knife through his heart. The Count was destroyed. Sadly, though, Quincey died — one of the Count's men had stabbed him. However, just before he died he saw that the red (**11**) .... on Mina's forehead had disappeared.

F ☐ Dr Seward still did not want to believe the horrible truth. They then went back to her (**12**) .... She was now in it. She was more beautiful than ever and had (**13**) .... teeth. This convinced Dr Seward. Van Helsing then explained that they had to (**14**) .... a stake through her heart to free Lucy. Two days later they told Arthur about everything, and that night they went back to find Lucy. Arthur hit the stake into Lucy, and in the end the (**15**) .... Lucy was there.

G ☐ The Count, they discovered, was travelling by river to his castle. They then divided up in three groups. Mina and Van Helsing travelled by train and then by (**16**) .... to the castle. That night the vampire women came and called to Mina. The next morning Van Helsing went into the castle and found the three vampire women. He then killed them.

H ☐ Then he heard Mina call him. He left the castle and they ran up on a hill. They saw the (**17**) .... carrying the Count in his box of earth. It was followed by Arthur, Jonathan, Dr Seward and Quincey on horses. The men escorting the Count tried to protect him, but Jonathan then threw the box to the (**18**) ....

I ☐ After her mother died, Lucy's condition got worse and worse. Then, when Van Helsing saw that the (**19**) .... on her neck had disappeared, he knew that she was dying. He called in Arthur. When Lucy saw Arthur she wanted to (**20**) .... him, but Van Helsing prevented her. At first she was very angry, but then she thanked Van Helsing and asked him to give her (**21**) .... She died soon afterwards.

③ Listening

FCE

You will hear Bram Stoker talking about his early childhood and some of the scary stories he heard — many of the elements of these stories were then imaginatively transformed in his novel *Dracula*. For questions, 1-10, complete the sentences.

1 Bram's mother and father always carried him around because he ....

2 Bram watched .... when he was in bed.

3 The people of Clontarf .... of people who committed suicide to keep them in the ground.

4 Bram's mother was just .... in 1832.

5 She came from Sligo, which is located ....

6 Some people drank .... in order not to die of hunger.

7 When you left somebody, you could not be certain that you would ....

8 In Bram's favourite story, a man managed to find his wife because she had ....

9   When Bram attended college in Dublin, he adored every
    ....

10 Bram still really likes ....

T: GRADE 7

4 Speaking: early memories

**As we heard in activity 3, Bram Stoker had a very unusual childhood.
Of course, many of the things he saw and heard remained with him
the rest of his life.**
Now make a short presentation about your early memories.
Use these questions to help you.

1   Has any event or person from your early childhood had a big
    influence on you?

2   What is your earliest memory?

 INTERNET PROJECT

Dracula was successful when it first appeared in 1897. It was also
successful as a play. But the influence of Count Dracula became
enormous with the arrival of films. From silent films to the first talking
pictures to the sophisticated computer-generated images of today,
Dracula and his descendants have appeared in hundreds and
hundreds of films. Some of them are truly wonderful and some of
them are truly terrible.
To find out more about these vampire films, connect to the Internet
and go to www.blackcat-cideb.com or www.cideb.it. Insert the title or
part of the title of the book into our search engine. Open the page for
Dracula. Click on the Internet project link. Go down the page until you
find the title of this book and click on the relevant link for this project.
You can even watch *Nosferatu: a Symphony in Horror*, the oldest
surviving film version of *Dracula*, and, according to many critics, the
best vampire movies ever.

Then make a short presentation about vampire films. Say:
▶ which ones look the scariest
▶ which ones look the strangest
▶ which one you think your class would like best and why
▶ why you think vampire films have been so popular.

133

Victorian Villains,
Monsters and Fears

Bram Stoker's great creation, the evil Count Dracula, was not just a pale, blood-sucking aristocratic vampire; he was also a great Romanian warrior. And, as is made clear in the novel, he is planning a massive invasion of England. Jonathan Harker himself realizes that the Count will create thousands and thousands of demons just like himself in London, in the heart of the British Empire. So, Stoker played with the fear of invasion of Britain. In literature this fear of invasion generally appeared with normal enemies as in the novel *The Battle of Dorking* (1871) by George Tomkyns Chesney, which gives a fictional account of a German invasion of Britain. Later H. G. Wells (1866-1946) imagined invaders from Mars in his frightening story *The War of the Worlds* (1898).

A fear that is closely related to that of invasion is the fear of foreigners who contaminate the purity of the 'British race'. This type of fear was very common in the late 1800s in all of Europe. One literary critic, Stephen D. Arata, called it the 'anxiety of reverse colonization'. In other words, just as the British brought their culture and customs to other countries, so people from other countries came to England. Or, there was the fear that the British in foreign lands would adopt native morals, ideals and customs. This was known at the time as 'going native'.

Both of these fears are not fears of being killed: they are fears of being transformed. This, of course, is exactly what Count Dracula does. His victims are not destroyed. They continue to exist but they too begin to suck blood and create more vampires. One of Stoker's models for

A scene from the silent film **The Phantom of the Opera** (1925),
directed by Rupert Julian.

Count Dracula was Svengali, an evil Jewish hypnotist from the 1894
novel *Trilby* by George du Maurier. This book takes place in the Paris
of the 1850s. With his hypnotic powers, Svengali turns the totally
unmusical Trilby O'Ferrall into a great singer called La Svengali. Like
Count Dracula, Svengali comes from 'the mysterious East, the
poisonous east.' Svengali also inspired another very popular literary
monster, the deformed Erik of the Paris Opéra in the 1910 novel *The
Phantom of the Opera* by Gaston Leroux (1868-1927).

Besides the general fear of invasions and of foreigners, Bram Stoker
played with the fear of the animal inside of each one of us. After the

great controversy surrounding the 1859 book *On the Origin of the Species* by the British naturalist Charles Darwin (1809-82), people became aware of our close ties with all other living things. For many people this created great anxiety and fear. They thought it showed that people were no better than animals or wild beasts. Stoker makes it clear that Count Dracula has very close ties to animals and that he himself is a kind of beast.

Another very popular book that played with this fear is *The Strange Case of Dr Jekyll and Mr Hyde* (1886) by Robert Louis Stevenson. In

Spencer Tracy as the young scientist in the film
Dr Jekyll and Mr Hyde (1941), directed by Victor Fleming.

Scene from the film **The Lost World** (1925), directed by Harry O. Hoyt.

this story Dr Jekyll discovers a way of bringing out his animal side and repressing his civilised side. Dr Jekyll's evil side is called Mr Hyde and he is similar to an ape. Another book with evil ape-men is *The Lost World* (1912) by Sir Arthur Conan Doyle (1859-1939). This book is about scientists who explore a mysterious plateau in the middle of the Amazon jungle. Dinosaurs still live on the plateau, but these terrible prehistoric lizards are not the real monsters of the book – the ape-men are. But, of course, as everybody knew after the publication of *On the Origin of the Species*, we all have a litte bit of ape in us.

Finally, Stoker played with the general fear of the 'new woman' (see page 91), and the sensuality and strength of women. All of the manly heroes in *Dracula* have trouble when they come face to face with the transformed women, the vampire women – even the great vampire hunter Van Helsing hesitates before the beauty of a female vampire. Another popular novel of that period dealing with dangerous females is the 1887 novel *She* by H. Rider Haggard (1856-1925). The 'She' of the title is short for 'She who must be obeyed', and she is Ayesha, the immortal white queen of an African tribe. Just like Stoker's horrible female vampires, Ayesha is both desired and feared by the men who see her.

So, we can see that in *Dracula* Bram Stoker succeeded in bringing together several of the main fears of his time. But these irrational fears, judging from the continued success of his novel, are also our own.

1 Comprehension check
Answer the following questions.

1 What do the novels *The War of the Worlds* and *Dracula* have in common?
2 What was the 'anxiety of reverse colonization'?
3 What does 'going native' mean?
4 Who is Svengali?
5 What monster, besides Dracula, was inspired by Svengali?
6 What fear was caused by Darwin's *On the Origin of the Species*?
7 Who is Mr Hyde?
8 Who is Ayesha?
9 What four fears did Stoker represent in his novel *Dracula*?

INTERNET PROJECT

H. G. Wells, the author of the novel *The War of the Worlds*, wrote another very influential novel that played on one of the great Victorian fears. This book has been made into three different films, and has had a large influence on books and films in general. To find out more about this frightening book, connect to the Internet and go to www.blackcat-cideb.com or www.cideb.it. Insert the title or part of the title of the book into our search engine. Open the page for *Dracula*. Click on the Internet project link. Go down the page until you find the title of this book and click on the relevant link for this project. With your partner prepare a short report about this book and the films based on it.

▶ When was the book published?
▶ What is it about?
▶ What particular Victorian fear does it deal with?
▶ When were the three films made?
▶ What famous actors were in them?
▶ Have you seen any films that seem similar to these films?

1 Picture summary

Look at the pictures from the story. Put them in their correct order by numbering them from 1 to 12 and write a caption under each one.

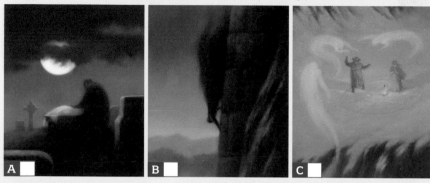

A ☐   B ☐   C ☐

D ☐   E ☐   F ☐

G ☐   H ☐   I ☐

 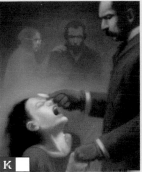 

2 **A graphic novel**

Photocopy these two pages, cut out the pictures and stick them on paper in the right order. Think of words to put in the balloons when the characters are speaking or thinking. Do not use the words that were used in this book! Then write at least a sentence under each picture to narrate what is happening.

3 **A quiz**

Did you enjoy *Dracula*? Here is a quiz about the story.
Answer the questions.

1   What did the landlady of the Golden Krone Hotel give Jonathan?

2   Who said the words 'the dead travel fast?'

3   What did Count Dracula do when he first met Jonathan?

4   What did the drivers take away from the Count's castle?

5   What was the *Demeter*, and what happened on it?

6   Why did Van Helsing decide to give Lucy a transfusion?

7   What did the Professor give Lucy instead of flowers?

8   What killed Lucy's mother?

9   What did Van Helsing promise Lucy that he would do?

10 Who or what was the 'bloofer lady?'

11 What happened to the children who disappeared?

12 What did Van Helsing place around the entrance of Lucy's tomb?

13 What did Arthur do to give Lucy peace?

14 What was Renfield's terrible dream about?

15 What did Mina do when the Holy Wafer touched her forehead?

16 What was the *Czarina Catherine*? What did it carry?

17 How many graves did Van Helsing find in the chapel?

18 What happened to Quincey?

19 What did he do before he died?

4 **Who am I?**

**Read the sentences and decide which character each one is about.
Write the letter of the right character next to the correct sentence.
You may use some characters more than once.
There is an example at the beginning (0).**

A Count Dracula   B Jonathan Harker

C Mina   D Lucy

E Van Helsing   F Renfield

G Quincey   H John Seward

I Arthur Holmwood

0 ...A..... I threw Jonathan's mirror out of the window.

1 .... I like animals, especially insects.

2 .... I sleepwalked when I was younger.

3 .... I've travelled all around the world and can speak American slang.

4 .... I'm the director of a lunatic asylum.

5 .... I went to Budapest to help Jonathan, who was ill.

6 .... I can climb down a wall quickly like a lizard.

7 .... I wrote everything happened to me on a notebook.

8 .... I know about every strange disease in the world.

9 .... I went with Van Helsing to see Lucy when Arthur told me that she was ill.

10 .... I kissed Lucy on her forehead before she died.

11 .... I was hypnotised by the Professor and said I could hear the sound of water.

12 .... I found the chapel where the Count's grave was.

13 .... I opened Lucy's tomb.

14 .... I loved Lucy but she refused to marry me.

15 .... One night I had a terrible dream about rats.

16 .... I liked walking in the churchyard with Lucy.

17 .... Three young women came to see me one night in the Count's castle.

18 .... I cut the Count's throat with a knife.

19 .... There is a red scar on my forehead.

20 .... I touched Mina's forehead with a Holy Wafer.

This reader uses the **EXPANSIVE READING** approach, where the text becomes a springboard to improve language skills and to explore historical background, cultural connections and other topics suggested by the text.

The new structures introduced in this step of our **READING & TRAINING** series are listed below. Naturally, structures from lower steps are included too. For a complete list of structures used over all the six steps, see *The Black Cat Guide to Graded Readers*, which is also downloadable at no cost from our website, www.blackcat-cideb.com or www.cideb.it.

The vocabulary used at each step is carefully checked against vocabulary lists used for internationally recognised examinations.

Step Four B2.1

All the structures used in the previous levels, plus the following:

Verb tenses
Present Perfect Simple: *the first / second* etc. *time that ...*
Present Perfect Continuous: unfinished past with *for* or *since* (duration form)

Verb forms and patterns
Passive forms: Present Perfect Simple
Reported speech introduced by precise reporting verbs (e.g. *suggest*, *promise*, *apologise*)

Modal verbs
Be / get used to + *-ing*: habit formation
Had better: duty and warning

Types of clause
3rd Conditional: *if* + Past Perfect, *would(n't) have*
Conditionals with *may / might*
Non-defining relative clauses with: *which*, *whose*
Clauses of concession: *even though*; *in spite of*, *despite*

Available at Step Four: